3/7/97

Dear Father Mahady,
                Just a
appreciation for all you have

                Thanks for

        lots of love,
                Gary and Tracy
                xxxx   —x—

WHITE HEAT

WHITE HEAT

The Leeds United Dream Team

JASON TOMAS

MAINSTREAM
PUBLISHING

EDINBURGH AND LONDON

First published in Great Britain in 1996 by
MAINSTREAM PUBLISHING COMPANY (EDINBURGH) LTD
7 Albany Street
Edinburgh EH1 3UG

ISBN 1 85158 886 8

All the photographs in this book are reproduced by kind permission
of Ross-Parry Picture Agency

A CIP catalogue record for this book is available from the British Library

Typeset by Bibliocraft, Dundee
Printed and bound in Great Britain by Butler & Tanner Ltd

Contents

1

John Charles

The late Don Revie has a lot to answer for.

Leeds United have been in existence for 77 years. But if one is looking to select a 'dream team' from all the great players they have had, it is difficult – and that's putting it mildly – to look beyond those who played for the club during Revie's 13 years as manager. Before he took over as player-manager in March 1961, Leeds, though possessing a reasonable sprinkling of exciting, top-class players from time to time, were no more than an average League club. This, indeed, was not a truly passionate football city. If anything, there was greater interest there in cricket and Rugby League, a situation Leeds did little to threaten before Revie took over. The only trophy they won was the Second Division title in 1924, and in the post-war pre-Revie years the biggest stir they caused was when they reached the FA Cup quarter-finals in 1950 and when they gained promotion to the First Division in 1956 and finished eighth the following season.

The post-Revie years have contained more appealing highlights, especially under the management of Howard Wilkinson and with the brilliance on the field of men like Gordon Strachan, Gary McAllister and Tony Yeboah. Under Wilkinson, Leeds won the Second and First Division Championships, and reached the League Cup final.

However, to think of the contenders for a best-of-all-time Leeds United line-up is immediately to evoke visions of Gary Sprake or David Harvey in goal; a defence of Paul Reaney, Jack Charlton, Norman Hunter and Terry Cooper; Billy Bremner, John Giles and Eddie Gray in midfield; and Peter Lorimer, Allan Clarke and Mick Jones up front. In other words, you think of the days when Leeds were one of the best teams in the world, with so many internationals in the squad that Leeds could easily have fielded two top teams.

You think of the Revie days. Under Revie, Leeds won the Championship and the Inter Cities Fairs Cup (UEFA Cup) twice, the FA Cup, and the League Cup. They were Championship runners-up five times, FA Cup runners-up three times and were also losing finalists in one European Champions Cup and one UEFA Cup. In their ten First Division seasons under Revie, the lowest position in which they finished was fourth.

However, as far as the pre-Revie years are concerned, there is one man who could be said to have brought as much excitement to the fans as Bremner and Co. His name is John Charles, the 'Gentle Giant' from Swansea who was an outstanding player at both centre-half and centre-forward, and who became an even bigger idol in the city of Turin during seven golden years with Juventus than he had been in Leeds.

Charles, in fact, was brought back to Leeds – by Revie – in August 1962, at the age of 30. It seemed an inspired move. With Leeds having finished the previous season near the bottom of the Second Division, and their average gate having slumped to 16,000, Revie noted that Elland Road was like a 'ghost town'. Who better to fire the imagination of the glamour-starved Leeds public, and provide the inspiration to lift Revie's team back into the First Division, than the great John Charles, the most complete player of his generation?

But the gamble failed. There is a world of difference between the approach of teams in the Italian top division and the English Second – this was certainly the case in those days –

and having spent so long in Italy, Charles found it difficult to readjust. At the time Revie bought him from Juventus for £53,000, he also signed a rather less well known Scottish striker by the name of Jim Storrie from Airdrie for £15,000. Yet while Storrie went on to become Leeds's leading scorer, with 25 goals in 36 matches, Charles lasted only three months at Leeds, playing just 11 matches before being transferred to another Italian club, Roma, for £65,000. Storrie recalls:

> Italian teams didn't do as much physical work in training as English sides and Charles no longer had the pace and stamina for the game in this country. I will always remember a match he played at Huddersfield. They gained possession and our forwards made their way back into covering positions. But when the ball was booted back into the Huddersfield half again, about ten seconds later, John was still in the process of getting back to the halfway line. He and Huddersfield's goalkeeper were the only players in that half of the field. One of the things we used to do in training was that eight or nine players would form a circle, with each one taking it in turns to come into the middle of it and give the rest an exercise to do. On his first day at Leeds, John did a sort of gentle warming-up exercise, which just involved running on the spot – light jogging on the spot would be a better way to describe it – and sort of twiddling his fingers at the same time. Les Cocker [Leeds's trainer] stopped him and asked him what he thought he was doing. John seemed to get quite indignant. 'Juventus won the Italian League and Cup on this stuff boy,' he said.

Revie himself, remembering the physical dynamism Charles displayed in his earlier period at Elland Road, quickly realised that he had made a mistake. During one of Charles's opening matches, he turned to Cocker and said: 'I don't think the big man can do it any more. He's gone.'

However, despite that unsatisfactory episode, and the fact that he has fallen on hard times in recent years, Charles's image in the eyes of the Leeds supporters has remained untarnished. To them, Charles is still 'King John' – a 6ft

2in, 14-stone colossus of a footballer and a sensitive, down-to-earth role model as a man. They take the view, with much justification, that Leeds would not have fallen into such gloomy times had they not let go of Charles, against his wishes, in the 1950s. In many ways, Charles was similar to Alan Shearer. As with Shearer before his world record £15 million move from Blackburn to Newcastle, Charles was very much at the top of the Leeds bill. When Leeds sold him to Juventus, also for a world record fee (£65,000), the sense of sadness at Elland Road was no less pronounced than it had been at Blackburn over Shearer's departure. Suffice it to say that Leeds's then chairman, Sam Bolton, was reported to be 'in tears'.

Charles's popularity owed as much to his temperament and personality as it did to his ability. It was rare that he lost his temper, although one who discovered that he could be pushed too far was Jack Charlton. Charles, having scored one of the goals that had given Leeds a 2–1 lead over Fulham, moved back to help his defence protect it in the last ten minutes. 'We don't want you up here,' Charlton told him. 'Get up the front where you belong.' One can only assume that the instruction, not unreasonable in itself, was couched in rather stronger terms than that. There had to be a good reason why, when Charlton was in the dressing-room bath afterwards, such a mild-mannered man as Charles should feel the need to grab him by the head and force it under water. Charles, the Leeds captain, recalls: 'I told him not to talk like that to me again and Jack said he was sorry. We're good friends actually.' Another player with the rare claim to fame of having incurred Charles's wrath was Austria's accomplished defender Ernst Ocwirk. Referring to Austria's 2–1 win over Wales at Wrexham in November 1955, Charles was once quoted as saying: 'I played a thousand matches as a professional footballer, Ocwirk was the one opposing player who made me lose my temper. It was the only time I went wild on a football pitch. Ocwirk kicked my brother Mel [the former Swansea, Arsenal, Cardiff and Port Vale centre-half] and I thought he had broken his leg. I charged up the field to get Ocwirk. If it hadn't been for somebody or something holding me back, I would have punched him. I never minded anyone kicking me and they did that often enough. I had six knee operations caused by kicks, but what happened to Mel that day made me mad.' Mel, who was out of the game for 14 weeks as a result of that tackle, confirmed this unusual occurrence. 'It was the only time I ever saw John get angry and raise his fists.'

It was a good thing that Charles did not get angry more often. His Leeds record speaks for itself. He scored 153 goals in 308 League matches, just 15 fewer than the only man above him on this list, Peter Lorimer, got in 525 games. Moreover, Charles, who made his debut for Leeds at 17 (and his debut for Wales at 18), played a number of his games at centre-half. What made Leeds's fortunes doubly difficult to take was the impact he had on Juventus. They had finished near the bottom of the table the season before he joined them, and in his first season he helped the Italian giants win the Championship. They won the title three times in all when he was there, and the Italian Cup. His claims to be recognised as the most successful of all the British footballers who have played for clubs abroad is further endorsed by the fact that he was selected for the Italian League representative team and was voted Italy's Footballer of the Year.

His presence in the Leeds team stemmed from the foresight of their manager, Major Frank Buckley, an authoritarian and unconventional figure who discovered the player when he was on the groundstaff of Swansea (Charles's home-town club) and signed him on his 16th birthday – 27 December 1949 – for ten pounds. It was a difficult move for Charles, a creature of habit who always tended to resist major upheavals in his life. Indeed, he says he would have been quite content to remain with Swansea, or anywhere in his beloved Wales, for that matter, had he been given more playing chances. 'I am one of those people who don't like moving from place to place, and I didn't want to go from Swansea,' he says. 'But the thing was, they didn't give me a chance. They didn't put me in their Welsh League team or their junior side – I was just doing jobs around the ground and training. Then, one day the manager said to me: "Would you like to go to England?" That was it. It was unbelievable; I'd never been outside Swansea and when I went home and told my mother, she says: "I think you'd have to have a passport." '

The decision earned him one of a different kind – a passport to fame and fortune. Leeds immediately put him into their Yorkshire League team, initially at left-back, then wing-half and finally centre-half. His first match for them in that position was at Bradford, a game in which Leeds had their first experience of the characteristics that were to lead to that 'Gentle Giant' tag. Charles recalls: 'Have you heard of Tom Farr [Bradford's goalkeeper from 1946 to 1949]? Well, when I went up for a corner, he smacked me around the jaw, and said to me: "Don't you come into the penalty area again." I said: "Mr Farr, I won't come in any more, don't you worry about that." I always remember that. I thought: "Bloody hell".' Farr must have done so, too, when just three months after joining Leeds Charles made his first-team debut at centre-half in a friendly match against Queen of the South, and had a more than useful game against their tough Scottish international centre-forward, Billy Houliston. He kept his place in the side. He was on his way to the top.

Buckley, in his sixties, and previously manager of Wolves, Notts County and Hull, must have represented an awesome figure to a youngster as raw and unworldly as Charles. Buckley's approach to the job was nothing if not unusual. A stickler for new ideas, he gave the Leeds players ballroom dancing sessions during training to help improve their balance. More controversial was his initiative in giving some players monkey gland extract, either through injections or tablet form, in the belief that it would sharpen their concentration. Above all, he had a strong personality, and was not averse to making full use of it. 'He would be sat in the stand during training, shouting instructions through a microphone,' Charles recalls. 'We used to get complaints from the residents of the estate across the road.' However, the major clearly thought the world of Charles, whom he rightly looked upon as his protégé, and Charles reciprocated this respect: 'He was a great man,' Charles says. 'I loved him, because I was one of his favourites. I think he thought: "Well, I've brought this young boy up from Swansea, I've got to look after him", and he did. He was a lovely man.' For his part, Buckley, a strict disciplinarian with a passionate belief in players forever striving to improve their ability, couldn't have failed to be impressed by Charles's enthusiasm, and willingness to learn. 'You've got to practise,' he points out. 'Even the most gifted players have to work at their games – they can't just rely on their natural ability. I was much better on my right side than the left, so for shooting practice, I'd have to wear a slipper on the left and nothing on the right and have to use the left all the time. That's the way we used to train.

'In them days, we had three months off in the summer, and you'd spend most of it working on things you weren't good at. One of my faults was that I couldn't jump very high, so every day for three months, I went back to the ground and practised by kicking the ball up against the stand and, no matter how it came off, trying to head the rebound in between two sticks. I put the sticks what seemed a mile apart at the start, but gradually reduced the space between them to the same size as the goal. By the end of those three months, I was able to get an average of eight goals from every ten attempts.'

It was in the FA Cup that Buckley's faith in Charles truly began to pay dividends; in the 1949/50 competition when Charles's ability at the back helped Leeds get to the quarter-finals for the first time in their history. After Carlisle had been despatched 5–2 in the third round, excitement in the city reached fever pitch as Leeds then overcame Bolton and Cardiff. Their reward was a glamorous quarter-final against Arsenal at Highbury, where Charles and his colleagues had the edge for most of the match but were sunk by a Reg Lewis goal a couple of minutes from the end. Lewis went on to score at Wembley to steer Arsenal to a 2–0 final victory over Liverpool.

But the future for Charles was even brighter, especially when Raich Carter, the brilliant former Sunderland and England inside forward, took over from Buckley as manager in 1953. Carter, much younger than Buckley at 40, was Charles's first 'track-suit' manager. Outside the Welsh squad, Carter, the youngest-ever captain of a Championship-winning team at Sunderland and part of a much-vaunted England forward line that also included Stan Matthews, Wilf Mannion, Nat Lofthouse and Tom Finney, was also the most illustrious professional he had worked with. Thus, as Carter was no shrinking violet when it came to talking about his past, Charles was given a mouth-watering insight into what life was like at the top level: 'On his first day, he called us into his office, told us to sit down, and then started showing us photographs of his playing career. "Look at that one," he was saying. "Wonderful picture ... that's when I scored a goal against so and so." He had all the pictures and he was telling us everything that had happened. He was like that, but he was a good man. He also liked playing Scottish teams. We played a lot of them when he was manager, and I think we must have been at the top of the Scottish League because we beat them all. It meant so much to him. Before we went out, he'd say: "Kill those Scottish bastards." I thought it was a bit strong – he didn't even know them – and I used to say: "But Raich, it's only a friendly." But it made no difference to him. "I don't care what it is," he'd reply. "We're going to beat them." He was unbelievable.'

The same could be said of Charles when Carter switched him to centre-forward for the manager's first season at Elland Road. Charles responded by scoring 42 League goals, a post-war club record, and an achievement that becomes even more impressive when you consider the quality of his team. For all Charles's power that season, Leeds could only finish tenth.

Two years later, Charles helped Leeds end a run of nine successive seasons in the Second Division and in their first season back – 1956/57 – he donned the striker's shirt again to propel them to eighth in the table. That was the season in which Charles produced the performances that he remembers the most – two League hat-tricks against Sheffield Wednesday. 'Six goals in two matches,' he muses, 'and outside sticking the ball in the net, I don't think I had a kick.' It was typical of Charles that he should be embarrassed enough by this even to apologise afterwards to the men who had been marking him.

For the first match, at Elland Road on 10 November, Charles, operating in a deep-lying role, was marked by Don Gibson, the son-in-law of Manchester United's manager Matt Busby. Leeds were a goal down after 15 minutes, and as the game progressed, Charles found it increasingly difficult to get into his stride. But after 35 minutes he got a goal out of the blue as a result of a Leeds free-kick from which Wednesday tried to catch Leeds offside. For once Charles, who had been snared in that offside trap earlier, did not fall for it; and when the ball broke to him, he was able to take it through, unchallenged, and put it in the net. That gave him all the encouragement he needed to destroy the opposition. After 51 minutes, he lost Gibson to run on to a delightful pass by Bobby Forrest and hit a 20-yard left-footed shot which went in off a post. Forrest, an inside forward who never seemed to stop running, and who later did much to bring out the best in those powerful strikers Jeff Astle and Tony Hateley at Notts County, also supplied the pass for Charles's third goal – a right-foot shot from 25 yards.

Because of his power in the air, Charles was also helped in those days by the service he was given from the flanks, from the Leeds wingers, George Meek and Jackie Overfield. This was underlined in the return match against Wednesday at Hillsborough on 25 March 1957 when these men set up a hat-trick of headed goals for Charles in a 3–2 Leeds win. Charles was marked by Andy McEvoy that day, and in the *Yorkshire*

Post report of the game, Eric Stanger wrote: 'Overfield vied with Alan Finney [the Wednesday winger] for star billing in this game, for Charles did not have much impact on the play. That was due in no small measure to McEvoy's watchfulness. He kept so close to Charles that he almost trod on his toes.' However, while that helped McEvoy when the ball was on the ground, it did not count for much when the ball was in the air – especially when two players who could strike the ball as accurately as Meek and Overfield were involved. Overfield, indeed, had a field day against the young Wednesday full-back, John Martin, who had come into the side as a result of an injury to their regular right-back Frank Staniforth. It was from Overfield's perfectly placed corner that Charles gave Leeds the lead with an equally impressive header after only three minutes. Wednesday then fought back to lead 2–1, but from a Meek cross, following an Overfield corner which had not been properly cleared, Charles made it 2–2 with a twisting header. Fifteen minutes from the end, Charles heaped further gloom on Wednesday – and McEvoy – when heading in another Overfield cross for the winner.

That season, his first in the First Division, Charles got 35 goals; and at the end of it, Leeds decided that the price Juventus were prepared to pay for him was too high to turn down. At the time of the £20-a-week maximum wage in English football, it was a wonderful deal for Charles, too. He received a £10,000 signing-on fee, and was paid twenty pounds a week, plus another twenty-five if Juventus won away from home and fifteen if they did so at home. It seems a pittance now, but in those days it was a fortune beyond most British players' wildest dreams.

Having settled down in Italy better than most people expected, he himself wanted to return to England in the early 1960s, because of his desire to return to his roots and have his children educated there. 'I probably should have stayed in Italy,' he says. 'But that's life, you know? You make mistakes in life.' It says much about Juventus's gratitude for the service he gave them that they still invite him back for special occasions. 'They had me over for the European Cup final [between Juventus and Ajax in 1996] and really looked after me. Everything was free – the travel expenses, hotel, everything. I think it is terrific that they still remember me. For me, that's what life is all about.'

In more recent years, Charles, who joined Cardiff after leaving Roma and then had spells as player-manager of Hereford, youth team coach at Swansea and manager of Merthyr, has been beset by financial problems. Yet, far from bemoaning his ill fortune, it still concerns him that he wasn't able to deliver the goods for the Leeds public in his second period with the club: 'I wouldn't have left Leeds in the first place had it been another British club. There was no point. I couldn't have earned any more at a place like Arsenal or anywhere else here than I was getting at Leeds, and not only this, I was happy at Leeds. I liked the people and I felt at home.

'The second time around, I like to think that, given time, I could have got back in the swing of things again, but it just didn't work out for me. I didn't feel good about that. You know what they [the Leeds board] did when I came back? They put half a crown on the admission prices. Some fans wanted to blame me, but I kept saying: "It isn't me. I have nothing to do with club policies." ' He shrugs, and adds: 'But they got over it, you know.' To those who remember performances like the ones he produced against Sheffield Wednesday, that is something of an understatement.

2

Norman Hunter

On 8 September 1962, Don Revie gathered four teenagers around him beneath the main stand at Swansea's Vetch Field ground and told them: 'You've got to do it for me today. My job is resting on your shoulders.' Three of the players, defenders Paul Reaney and Norman Hunter (a month short of their 18th and 19th birthdays) and striker Rod Johnson (17) were making their Leeds League debuts; the other, goalkeeper Gary Sprake (also 17), had made only one previous first-team appearance, as an emergency replacement for the injured Tommy Younger six months earlier. The decision to throw them all into the deep end of senior professional football at the same time was worrying even to Revie. 'I know I have made mistakes but I think I might have done something really bad this time,' he confided to the Leeds chairman, Harry Reynolds, on the eve of the match. 'I have put in four kids who are just not ready for this level of football. If things go wrong for them, it could ruin their confidence. It could have a disastrous effect on their whole careers.'

However, desperate situations call for desperate measures. Leeds, then in the Second Division, had twice come close to relegation to the Third since Revie became player-manager in March 1961. They eventually finished the 1960/61 season in 14th position, and the following season, when they had to wait until the last Saturday to make themselves safe from the drop – through a remarkable 3–0 win at Newcastle – they were 19th. The start of the 1962/63 season offered little prospect of a change in their fortunes. They won only two of their first six games, three of which were lost, and the seventh, at Swansea, had been preceded by a dismal 2–1 home defeat by Bury. However, his gamble on Sprake, Reaney, Hunter and Johnson paid off because Leeds won 2–0, and Revie was able to look back on that match as the turning point of his managerial career. 'Those lads breathed new life into the side,' Revie said.

With Sprake, Reaney and Hunter, they certainly breathed new life into the Leeds defence. Leeds lost only ten of their remaining 35 League matches that season to finish fifth. It was from that point that Leeds's image as the most Scrooge-like team in Britain was truly born. There were only three defeats, and just 34 goals conceded, when they won the Second Division Championship the following season, and only two defeats and 26 goals conceded (both club records) when they won the Championship for the first time in 1968/69. Of course, in all good teams defending is a collective responsibility, one that is shared not just by the goalkeeper and his back-line colleagues, but also the midfielders and strikers. In that respect, the clearest visions of Leeds at their defensive best concern the remarkable show of bloody-minded defiance that enabled them to draw 0–0 with Ferencvaros in Budapest at the start of that 1968/69 season, and thus win the European Fairs Cup; and again in their last match of the season, when another epic backs-to-the-wall battle at Liverpool gave them the goalless draw that enabled them to clinch the title.

If there is one man who epitomised this side of Leeds, it was Hunter. Indeed, when you think of what Leeds United were like in those days, the first image that springs to mind is of Hunter's unfailing determination and concentration – and, of course, the bone-shaking tackles (not to mention fouls) that put him in the same macho category as Liverpool's

Tommy Smith, Manchester United's Nobby Stiles, Chelsea's Ron Harris and Arsenal's Peter Storey and led to those famous terrace banners proclaiming 'Norman bites yer legs'.

As with all the game's hard men, Hunter, who played for Leeds for 14 years, seemed as placid off the field as he was aggressive on it, and had more ability than he was often given credit for. The Leeds player with the fourth highest number of first-team appearances – 726, behind Jack Charlton, Billy Bremner and Reaney – he was arguably the one who achieved the highest level of consistency. It is also reasonable to suggest that Hunter would have gained many more than his 38 England caps but for the fact that his career coincided with that of Bobby Moore. As it was, the only member of the Leeds back four who played for England more times than he did was Charlton, and even he only did so seven more times.

Though Hunter and Charlton were both born and raised in the north-east – in Eighton Banks, County Durham, and Ashington, Northumberland respectively – they had very little else in common. Charlton, ten years older than Hunter, was an established member of the Leeds team at 27 when Hunter started operating alongside him at the heart of the Leeds defence. In addition to his greater experience, he had a stronger personality than Hunter, and had formed much stronger views on how he and the game generally should be played. Charlton was nothing if not headstrong and stubborn, a trait which made him something of a late developer as a top-class player. With Hunter, the reverse was true. Indeed, while Hunter rightly singles out Charlton as having a big influence on his progress in the game, it is tempting to suggest that the presence of a youngster as disciplined and steady as Hunter was helpful to Charlton, too.

Prior to the period in which Hunter made his mark, Leeds had been having problems with Charlton. Revie recalled that when he first started working with Charlton, the centre-half had the 'irksome habit' of venturing upfield to try and get a goal at the wrong times, leaving his defence exposed. Jim Storrie, one of Leeds's strikers, had this to say about it:

> Jack had been playing the game his way for so long that he found it difficult to accept his way was wrong. Don [Revie] wanted Jack to stick to the opposing centre-forward everywhere he went in our half of the field, but this was foreign to Jack. He preferred to stay where he was, in the middle, so that he could head the ball away if the winger got in a cross. What was happening, however, was that people were coming off Jack, turning, and either taking him on or going past him by playing one-twos. Time and again, Don said to him: 'You've got to make sure that the centre-forward can't turn with the ball and come at you.' Then, Jack started going halfway, which was even worse. If the centre-forward ran 20 yards off Jack to collect a pass, Jack would go ten yards. So he was being stranded in no man's land.
>
> Jack could be very stubborn. He wouldn't accept the blame for anything. If he landed on his backside, and his opponent went on to score, he would probably claim that it was the fault of one of the Leeds forwards for having lost possession 50 yards up the field, or something like that.

Not surprisingly, this aspect of Charlton's character led to some interesting dressing-room showdowns. The one that Revie himself remembered the most was when Leeds lost 2–1 at Rotherham in January 1962 through a last-minute goal which he deemed to have been caused by a Charlton mistake. In the dressing-room afterwards, the dispute between the two over this became so heated that Charlton angrily threw a glass against the wall.

According to Storrie, Charlton started to come to terms with what was expected of him after a 2–2 draw at Luton, a couple of weeks after Hunter's Leeds debut: 'They [Luton] were awarded a free-kick just outside our area, and as the fellow took the kick, Jack screamed "Out!" [an instruction to the other defenders to move forward to catch Luton offside]. Well, everyone ran forward, but Jack stayed, and Luton equalised. Don blew a fuse with him afterwards, but when everyone had calmed down, he said: "Look, Jack, if you are drawn out of the middle and we concede a goal, I will exonerate you from all blame. As long as you are standing with their centre-forward, I will be happy." That was right up Jack's street. From then on, he started to track the centre-forward, and Leeds started going places.

'I have nothing but admiration for the way that Jack changed, and emerged as an international-class centre-half. It spoke volumes for his character.'

That word 'character', when applied to honesty, represented the guiding light for youngsters such as Hunter. 'Don was always stressing the importance of players being honest with each other, and not being afraid to own up to mistakes,' Storrie says. 'He ended up with some of the youngsters in the team taking it too literally. When we gave away a silly goal, they would all be claiming responsibility for it. It was quite funny really, seeing the lads putting their hands up and giving all sorts of strange, obscure reasons to support their claims.'

Hunter smiles over the memory – and reminds you that Big Jack, his bolshie big brother-figure, never did change totally:

> He still had this bee in his bonnet about not wanting to leave the middle. I remember a game against Sheffield Wednesday, when Jack has drifted into another area and their big centre-forward [John Ritchie] has got above me to head a cross into the net. 'You see?' Jack said. 'Every time I go away a goal goes in. I'm staying here from now on.' Sometimes, he stood there like a policeman on traffic duty. I can see it to this day, big Jack just standing in the middle and telling everyone where to go. He'd have us running around all over the place. 'Go get him, Norm . . . Paul [Reaney] here . . . Pick him up Gilesey . . .' But I tell you what – when the ball was put into that box, he didn't half clear it. When it came to attacking the ball in the air, he was the best centre-half I ever played with. There was nobody better, especially when he was fired up. If somebody annoyed him, oh big Jack was superb.

The other Charlton picture in Hunter's mind concerns his clashes with Sprake, on the occasions that the keeper let in soft goals. 'For about two or three years, he slaughtered all of us, not just Sprakey,' Hunter recalls. 'But it was good for us youngsters to have someone getting on to us. Then, once you become established as a first-team player, you started having a go back at him. The great thing about the big man was that he never ever held a grudge. You could have some right humdingers with him on the pitch, but Jack – well, he would never say he was sorry, mind you, but if you apologised, he would say: "Oh, it's all right, man, it happens." That was it, finished.'

Hunter could also be seen apologising to opponents – the ones knocked over by one of his renowned crunching tackles. One arm would be raised, as if to acknowledge that maybe he had allowed his combativeness to run away with him, and this would invariably be followed by a disarming 'Who, me?' smile as the referee reached for his yellow card. Hunter has mixed feelings about the reputation this gave him. He argues that it was defenders like him who helped make the forwards of his era so skilful, and the game exciting: 'In my day, everybody knew that the first tackle you made was going to be made with the intention of letting the forward know you're there. I always felt that if they lay down and didn't come back at you again, it would make my afternoon very easy, but that if they jumped up and came back at me, then you've got a game of football. That was the norm, wasn't it? I mean, when I watch some of the old matches on TV – the 1970 Chelsea–Leeds FA Cup final, for example – I always wonder what today's referees would make of it? There were loads of hefty tackles, people being whacked all over the place, but the players just got up and got on with it, and the crowd loved it.'

That is not to say that Hunter does not look back on some of his more zealous challenges without a degree of embarrassment. He insists, with much justification, that they stemmed from his inbuilt competitiveness and enthusiasm for the game, and more pertinently his anxiety about letting his team down, than any real malice. He puts it this way: 'I look back, and I think: "I didn't do that, did I?" You know, you don't realise some of the tackles you do. I used to get quite surprised, genuinely surprised, when I was booked sometimes. I remember Paul Madeley and I were once playing together in a representative match, and me getting booked for the second of two "foul" tackles which I thought were perfectly OK. I protested to the ref, and Paul says: "You really don't think you have done anything wrong, do you?" I says: "No," and he says: "You absolutely buried that fellow – you took the ball, him, the lot." Even at Bristol City [where he ended his playing career], when I saw some of the tackles I made when I was with them, on a film they showed me, my reaction was: "Where did you get those from?" '

It is ironic that Hunter should have provoked such trepidation among opponents, given his average physique. At one time, Leeds had doubts about whether he would be strong enough to make the grade with them. 'Jack Taylor was manager when I signed for Leeds, and he didn't really fancy me. On my 17th birthday, he said that he didn't think I was big and strong enough, but that he would keep me for another six months and see what happened. Then, fortunately for me, Don Revie took over as manager. I am quite slim to this day, but you see the thing is, I am very bony. If I used to catch someone, with an elbow or a knee, it used to really hurt them. The only thing the gaffer did with me was make sure I ate sherry and eggs. I hated that – didn't like sherry – but on the gaffer's instructions, my mum would have to mix two eggs with the sherry and give it to me each morning. He also used to send steaks to the house for me.'

More important was what was already inside Hunter's heart and soul. 'I don't know why, but I was always a good winner of the ball – I always wanted to win the ball. I was more of a wing-half or a midfield player when I joined Leeds, but I'd always find myself being drawn back deep into our own half and getting my foot in.' Hunter's competitiveness was such that he was one of the Leeds players who suffered most from nerves before a game. 'Once we were on the field, I was OK. It was just the build-up to it. I wasn't as bad as Sprakey [he was physically sick before games] but I did get het up about it. I never wanted to play badly, you see – that was the thing that worried me more than anything. John Giles used to keep saying to me: "Just calm down, Norm," but I still got myself in a state. I'm the same now. Before I get up to talk [on his after-dinner speaking engagements] I'm very nervous.'

In one sense, Hunter had good cause to be that way as a Leeds player, especially in the days when Leeds were labelled too negative. In their first season back in Division One, for example, extra pressure was put on the defence because of the team's inexperience, and the fact that they did not have as many top-quality attacking players as other sides. Hunter, recalling the FA Cup final against Liverpool when Leeds fought back from a goal down but lost in extra-time, says: 'We defended well – we had to, because Liverpool battered us – and when Billy [Bremner] scored the equaliser near the end of normal time, I think Liverpool had gone. We should have gone after them, but we didn't have the know-how.' Leeds did become more assertive, but to Hunter, there were still times when they did not impose themselves as much as he felt they could have done. 'I don't know why, but once we were one-up, then instead of going for two or three and making the game easy for ourselves, we would shut up shop. All right, it worked for us, but a number of matches turned out to be unnecessarily hard for us as a result of our sitting back and inviting the opposition on to us.'

With a back four of Reaney or Madeley at right-back, Charlton and Hunter in the middle and Terry Cooper at left-back, it was little wonder that Revie felt 'as if I could light a cigar and relax'. It wasn't always like that, of course. There were the odd occasions when Revie will have been moved to replace that cigar with a stiff brandy. Hunter recalls that Stoke were something of a bogey team to the Leeds defence: 'They used to cause us a lot of problems, especially when Peter Dobing [their astute centre-forward] was playing. They had a skilful team who just went out and played. They had the confidence to have a go at us. That was probably the best way to beat us – well, it is the way to beat most sides, but a lot of teams used to come to Elland Road and just sit there. I've seen teams beaten by us before they've even got off the coach, you know what I mean?'

Leeds must have wished they had stayed in their own vehicle when they played a League Cup tie at West Ham at Upton Park on 7 November 1966. They had conceded only one goal in their three previous ties, and beaten Arsenal 1–0 at Highbury in their last First Division match. But West Ham thrashed them 7–0 – their worst post-war defeat.

Though the Hammers' left winger, John Sissons, scored a hat-trick, the man who did most of the damage to the Leeds defence was Johnny Byrne, a quick, ingenious centre-forward who repeatedly moved off Charlton to receive the ball and orchestrate his team's final thrusts for goal. Hunter, too, had a bad time: 'I was marking a lad called Peter Brabrook [West Ham's outside right]. He was a lad who could catch pigeons.' Leeds were hardly the sort of team to adopt a philosophical attitude to such a defeat, especially after the experience that Revie had when he sought out West Ham's manager, Ron Greenwood, to congratulate him on his team's performance. Unlike Revie, Greenwood was not an emotional man. Referred to as 'The Professor' because of his erudite, scholarly manner, he could be disconcertingly controlled in his reaction to his team's great moments. On this occasion, Revie interpreted it as arrogance. 'When I went into the West Ham dressing-room to congratulate him,' Revie recalled, 'he was so aloof towards me that I almost felt I had to pick his hand up to shake it.' Revie then stormed back into the Leeds dressing-room, slammed the door behind him, and told his players: "I would hate to see us beaten by that man's team again." Significantly, the only other occasion that Leeds lost to West Ham under Revie's management came in 1974, shortly before his departure from the club to take on the England job. The other matches between the two teams produced seven Leeds wins and six draws, and the total number of goals they conceded over those 15 First Division clashes was no more than 13.

West Ham were in good company, though; if any team could be expected to break the hearts of opposing strikers, it was Leeds. One of the great things about having Hunter operating at the heart of their defence was his discipline, his dogged determination to stick to what were perceived as his strengths. While some defenders can get bored just hanging around at the back, watching the men in front of them having fun with the ball, Hunter was mostly content with his lot. He could control and pass the ball as well as most defenders, as he emphasised in the 1972 FA Cup final against Arsenal by winning a tackle and then surprisingly dribbling around two Arsenal defenders, in the tightest of areas. Though some argued that he was too one-footed, this criticism counted for little when you saw balls being played to his right and, no matter what their height or speed, Hunter still being able to take them with his left. But Hunter's biggest strength was his ability to win the ball, and his willingness to release it as quickly and simply as possible:

> Well it did slightly annoy me at times [the fact that he couldn't 'play' more]. But, when you looked at the players I had in front of me, you have to say that was right. I don't know how Billy [Bremner] and Gilesey kept finding the space, but nine times out of ten, they'd be there demanding the ball from me before I could even think of doing something more adventurous with it. They were both so hungry for the ball. If I passed the ball to the Irishman [Giles], the Scotsman [Bremner] told me off; if I passed to the Scotsman, the Irishman told me off. But it was mostly Gilesey who was there. After winning the ball, the

first thing you heard was: 'Yes, Norm.'

It was just so easy for me. Apart from Gilesey and Bremner, I could knock the ball over to the right, for Paul Reaney or Peter Lorimer, I could play it wide on my side to Terry Cooper and Eddie Gray – God almighty, as a defender trying to get rid of the ball to someone who could do something with it, I was really in trouble, wasn't I? With TC [Cooper] and Eddie [Gray] I felt like saying: 'There you are lads, there's the ball – and can I have it back, please, when you get fed up with it?' Les Cocker [Leeds's trainer] used to describe the three of us as the Three Ringed Circus.

However, when it came to expressing creative skills, Hunter was very much the supporting act in that trio. He has a particular respect for Cooper, a former outside left who emerged at Leeds as one of the best attacking left-backs in the world. Cooper, Hunter's room-mate, was a player who could even be described as a kindred spirit. Hunter says of him:

People used to say: 'Oh, he can only go forward,' but he could defend as well you know. He was a tough little fellow. I'll never forget the day he lost his teeth. Paul Madeley was at centre-half and Paul, me and TC all jumped for this ball. Big Paul got it away, and then came over to me and showed me his arm. 'Look at this,' he says – he had deep teeth marks on his elbow. Anyway, shortly afterwards I knocked the ball out to TC and, strangely for him, he mis-hit it into the crowd. I said: 'You all right, pal?' Then I saw that two of his front teeth were missing and that two others were just hanging on by bits of skin. What a state he was in. But what a great player he was. I would get the ball, and go boomph. 'There you are TC, off you go.'

People get on to me about Leeds's so-called regimented style of play. They say: 'You were very well-drilled' and all that. But the truth is that we were never really coached as much as people thought we were. We reached a stage where all we had to do was keep ourselves fit. I believe to this day that if you have good players, and they have done their warm-ups, their stretching exercises, etc, then you can get all the 'coaching' you need simply by playing in five-a-sides and practice matches. You know, the overlaps I used to do, where I'd go around

the back of TC or Gilesey – people said: 'Oh, you must have
spent hours on that,' but no, it just happened. It was the same
with big Jack standing on the opposing goal-line for corners
and free-kicks. There was a corner in a practice match; Jack
wandered up the field and stood under the crossbar; Eddie
Gray curled the kick under the bar; and Jack went, bang – it
was in the net. So then they got a free-kick on the other flank
[taken by Lorimer], Jack went up again – boomph, another
goal. So obviously, Jack started doing it in matches, but it was
never planned.

In addition to his heading ability, the 6ft 1in Charlton also
made a big impression on Hunter with the speed with which
those long legs of his covered the ground, and his ability to keep
his shots low, all of which brought Charlton 75 goals compared
with Hunter's total of 21. Still, at least Hunter did better in
that department than Cooper (11) and Reaney (7); and, for
all the criticism he attracted through his hard-man image, he
had the backing of the two managers he most admired: Revie
and his England boss, Sir Alf Ramsey.

Hunter found them quite similar, in terms of their attention
to detail, the discipline they imposed, and the loyalty
and support they showed to their players. Ramsey would
occasionally chastise Hunter, albeit gently, over his physical
approach to the game, his willingness to take on the physical
battles of his team-mates as well as his own: 'He used to come
up and have a quiet word with me about it,' Hunter recalls.
'He'd say: "Why do you do these sort of things, you're too good
a player to do things like that." I'd say: "Well, it's part of being
a Leeds United player – you don't like getting beaten, and you
don't like people taking liberties with one of your players." I
don't know whether Alf really accepted this, but what I do
know is that, publicly, he supported you to the hilt. I worked
with him for nine years, and I thought he was a lovely man.
With Bobby [Moore] around, I knew that I would spend most
of my time on the England bench but this didn't matter to me. I
wanted to keep being part of the squad as much because of Alf

as I did because of the personal prestige of it. You talk to any of the England players who worked with him; you'll find that not one has a bad word to say about him, not one.' The same applies to Revie: 'You had total and utter respect for him. I was going to say that the players feared him, but it was respect more than anything else. It was amazing, I was only late for training once, and I remember him just coming up to me and looking at his watch. That was all he did, and all he needed to do to make you feel bad. But the way he supported you, stuck by you, was something else. You know, I'd got this hard-man image and there were times when I was getting so much stick . . . but he used to say to me: "You go out and do what you're good at and I will take care of everything else." He was happy to take the stick I got onto his shoulders – he protected you in so many ways. As far as I was concerned, what he said was law.'

The respect was mutual. On the subject of Norman Hunter, Revie was liable to deliver the equivalent of a Churchillian speech. This was particularly true when it came to Leeds's big European cup battles on foreign territory. The heavier the fire, the more Hunter and Charlton could be relied upon to show why any manager worth his salt would have been happy to be sitting beside them in the 'trenches'. Significantly, these are the matches which Hunter remembers the most. 'I loved the European ties, absolutely loved them. They were a refreshing change from the Championship and FA Cup matches. You were playing against totally different players, many of whom you'd never heard of, and the atmosphere was electric. Oh, we had some great games in Europe – great results.'

Epic battles, too. His favourites all took place in the Fairs (UEFA) Cup. One was in the third-round first-leg tie against Valencia at Elland Road on 2 February 1966 – a 1–1 draw in which Charlton and two Valencia players were sent off, and the referee took both teams back to the dressing-room for a cooling-down period. Every time Charlton had taken up that favourite position of his on the opposing goal-line, he'd been subjected to niggling intimidatory digs and shoves. Finally, 17 minutes from the end, Charlton, kicked as he challenged for a high ball, and then punched, finally exploded. 'Oh, it was the funniest thing you'll ever see,' Hunter says, clearly relishing the gladiatorial nature of the scene. 'I think it was the keeper who punched him, because all of a sudden, you could see this keeper running around the back of the goal and the big man chasing after him.' In the ensuing chaos – in which Charlton was able to land some blows of his own – the police came onto the pitch and the referee, the famous Dutchman Leo Horn, walked off with his linesmen and signalled to the officials of the two clubs to bring their players off as well.

Horn sent word into the dressing-rooms that Charlton and Valencia's left-back, Garcia Ridagany, someone else with whom the centre-half had crossed swords, had been sent off; and not long after play resumed, Valencia's inside forward, Lage, was banished too.

Not many players in Leeds's position would have relished the return leg in Valencia, in front of 45,000 of the most hostile fans in Europe. Trust Leeds, though, to be more bloody-minded than ever and win 1–0.

To Hunter, the atmosphere of hate in that contest was nothing compared to the mood he experienced in the second-round, second-leg tie against Napoli in Naples on 27 November 1968 when Leeds, 2–0 up from the first leg, were 2–0 down (2–2 on aggregate) after extra-time. 'It was the only time I was ever frightened on a football field,' Hunter says. 'One Napoli player stuck the head on Mick O'Grady and the crowd were so hostile, it wasn't true. We had bottles raining down on us – everything. We were keeping our cool quite well, but right at the end of normal time, this big winger jumped at Paul Madeley and caused a horrible cut on Paul's thigh. Now, you know what the big man was like – he didn't hurt anyone, did he? – and the gaffer was more upset than anyone over the challenge. So much so that, when the final whistle went, and he got us all together [to give advice and instructions for the extra-time period], he said: "Right, that's it. I don't care about the result – just bury them." It was the only time I ever heard the gaffer say something like that. Well, for that extra-time, it was war, absolute war.' It was also a great night for Leeds, result-wise: with the aggregate score at 2–2, they got through to the next round on the toss of a coin.

However, the mother and father of all Leeds's European cup battles, and the one that perhaps best encapsulated the qualities Hunter brought to the side, took place in September of that year – the 0–0 draw against Ferencvaros in Hungary which made them the first British team to win the trophy. At that time, Hungarian football, renowned for its attacking flair, was going through a good spell. Ferencvaros themselves were looked upon as one of the most potent attacking teams in the world, let alone Europe. They had Albert, one of the stars of the 1966 World Cup finals, for a start. Then there was Varga, a supremely gifted young ball-playing inside forward, and the experienced left-wing pair of Rakosi and Fenyvesi.

It came as a surprise in the first leg at Elland Road when Ferencvaros showed a more ruthless side to their game, physically and tactically. They might well have got the goalless draw they sought but for the unease of their goalkeeper Geczi in dealing with balls in the air. Hunter had an outstanding chance when Geczi missed a cross early in the match; the ball ran straight to his feet, just ten yards out, but the defender was so surprised by his good fortune that he mis-hit his shot wide. Another mistake by Geczi, albeit one that could be attributed to his defenders restricting his space in their anxiety about Charlton on the goal-line, led to Leeds going ahead just before half-time. Geczi could only get his fingertips to a Lorimer corner from the right, and Jones was on hand to hit the loose ball into the net.

But it was a rather different Ferencvaros in the famous Nep Stadium in Budapest, where that attacking magic, before a crowd of 76,000, was turned on to full volume; and Leeds had to produce one of the all-time great shows of defiance to prevent themselves being obliterated. There was an added political twist to the occasion, as Leeds were the first foreign team to visit a Warsaw Pact country following Russia's invasion of Czechoslovakia. On the day of the game, Phil Brown in the *Yorkshire Evening Post* proved impressively prophetic when he wrote: 'Hungarian newspapers, Hungarian officials and Ferencvaros supporters all make a big point that their pair of famous strikers, Albert and Varga, will not be "under wraps" as they were at Elland Road, where they certainly showed restraint in attack. These two are among the best in the world on top form. I saw them riddle Brazil in the 1966 World Cup, and if they hit it tonight, Leeds are in trouble – but no more trouble than Albert and Varga would be if United turn in one of their "they shall not pass" displays, with Bremner, Charlton and Hunter reaching the heights they reached before in United's battles on the Continent.' As Brown wrote afterwards: 'The secret of United's success against a better team was I think simply their sheer never-give-up spirit in defence. They were always there when it came to the key moment, when the shots or the headers were to be taken. Nobody shirked a thing, even when lungs and legs were straining against the onslaught.'

Every Leeds player reached those heights. Sprake had probably his finest match for Leeds, pulling off one mind-boggling save from an explosive 20-yard free-kick from Ferencvaros's captain, Novak, and on another occasion when Ferencvaros looked certain to score, Cooper made an acrobatic overhead goal-line clearance from Rakosi. However, it said much about the concentration and tenacity of the likes of Hunter that, for the most part, Ferencvaros created fewer clear-cut scoring chances like these than one might have expected of a team having virtually all the attacking play. It also emphasised how quickly the likes of Hunter had absorbed their previous European lessons. In that respect, John Giles, who missed the match because of an injury, said:

When watching it on TV, I couldn't help thinking back to another Fairs Cup match against a Hungarian team, Ujpest Dozsa in 1966. Hungarian players are all particularly adept at playing quick one-twos in front of goal; their sharpness and control in tight areas is remarkable and they can go through you like a knife cutting butter. When facing this style of play, it is essential for defenders to stick close to their opponents and not be lured into chasing after the ball. Leeds made this error against Ujpest when we played them in Hungary. We escaped with a 1–1 draw to go through to the next round 5–2 on aggregate, but the way they passed their way through and around our defenders, we could have had no complaints had we been crushed. This was where the performance against Ferencvaros was so special. The discipline of people like Norman Hunter, their ability to read the game, meant that for all the pressure Ferencvaros exerted, they rarely got a man 'free' in our penalty areas.

'When we got into those final few minutes [when Ferencvaros threw everything but the proverbial kitchen sink at Leeds] my heart nearly stopped beating,' Revie said. Hunter, though, was in his element. There was a battle to be won – in its way the toughest battle of his life – and he was loving every second of it.

3

Paul Reaney

When George Best was in his pomp, there was hardly a full-back in Britain, or Europe for that matter, who relished the challenge of facing the brilliant Manchester United and Northern Ireland winger. The one exception was Leeds United's Paul Reaney. In fact, during Best's 12-year career at Old Trafford (1963–1975) one could even go as far as to say that he was more nervous about Reaney than vice versa.

Leeds and Manchester United had a number of epic battles in those days; quite apart from their First Division tussles, the two teams – whose rivalry was similar to that of Manchester United and Newcastle today – had two FA Cup semi-final clashes in 1965, and three in 1970. Best, though, has good cause to want to forget them because, due to Reaney's pace, athleticism and concentration, he was hardly allowed a kick of the ball. Needless to say, three of those matches were goalless draws, and Leeds won the other two 1–0. Perhaps the most vivid illustration of Reaney's effect on Best came on one of the few occasions that he did manage to break free of him, in the first 1970 semi-final replay at Villa Park, when Best bore down on the Leeds goal and had only the keeper, Gary Sprake, to beat. Best, no doubt surprised that he had got into this position, then trod on the ball and the chance was lost.

More recently, Reaney himself was taken aback by Best

when the two men met at a holiday camp at Bognor, where Reaney was coaching schoolboy players and Best was taking part in a football forum. They'd hardly said two words to each other when they were players, but Best, on catching sight of Reaney, walked across to him and put his arms around him like a long-lost brother. 'I couldn't believe it,' Reaney recalls. 'I said: "George, is this you?" I don't know – he'd had one or two [drinks], so maybe that explained it.'

It was less difficult to fathom why Reaney, unlike most other full-backs, was able to play some of the best matches of his long Leeds career against Best. Part of the reason concerned the nature of his role against Best. Defenders in British teams usually adhere to a zonal marking system; they cover areas of the pitch as opposed to specific opponents. In normal circumstances, Reaney would only have been expected to be in close contact with Best had the winger come into his zone. If Best had moved into a deeper position on the right, or drifted inside, he would have been 'passed on' to another Leeds player. But on most of the occasions Leeds played Manchester United, Reaney was assigned to stick like glue to Best wherever he went in the Leeds half. As Reaney says: 'It reduced the matches to ten against ten. When Leeds got the ball, I was too close to George to get many touches, and the same applied to him when Manchester United got the ball.'

Reaney was also helped by the fact that he was able to gain a psychological edge on Best:

> I think that it [his success against Best] just built up in his mind. It's natural, isn't it? I'd have been the same in his position. Every time you are about to play Leeds, you are thinking: 'Oh no, he is going to be there again. I don't fancy it.' So I used to play a bit on that, yeah. You could smell it.
>
> He was laughing at me once, when he scored against us [in the League match at Old Trafford at the end of the 1965/66 season]. But then I got our equaliser, which was unusual for me because if there's one thing I didn't do very well during my career it was score goals. He could do everything, Best,

but to be fair, I had the speed to keep up with him, and the concentration to avoid buying any of his dummies and things like that. It was being able to keep close to George that did it for me, and I was quite physical with him. That doesn't sound very nice, I know, but any winger knows that when it's a fifty-fifty ball, and he's got someone as close to him all the time as I was, then he's going to get cracked to a certain extent. I am not saying I played dirty against him, but I had to let him know that I wanted that ball more than he did.

He was so sick to death of me once that he turned around and clouted me. It was really funny; I wasn't really expecting it, and the first person to come over me to me was Norman Hunter, who told me to go into a different position. He said: 'Paul, you just go over there a minute,' and he stood right in front of George as if to say: 'Well, you've got me now.' Frightening.

If Best was intimidated by this, then he was hardly alone. When the going got tough, the Leeds defence got going. When riled, they took no prisoners. In his own case, Reaney recalls a clash with Chelsea's winger Peter Houseman at Stamford Bridge. 'The ball was running over the goal-line and, with no chance of getting it, he kind of did me on the ankle. Les Cocker [the trainer] came on but when he asked me how bad it was, and whether I should come off, all he was getting out of me was: "You've got to give me another 20 minutes . . . just give me another 20 minutes." Ten minutes later, I did something that I shouldn't have done and as he was on the ground, Houseman just looked up at me and said: "I'll never do that again." It wasn't nice what I did, but an eye for an eye I suppose. In matches at Elland Road, there were so many left wingers who said to me: "I'll be glad when this game is over." Not George, but quite a few others. We would be two up, and you knew that all that side wanted to do was get off the park. It doesn't half build you up.'

Generally, the Houseman incident apart, Reaney was no football assassin. In a career spanning 20 years, he was never sent off and was booked no more than five times – three when playing against Sunderland's George Mulhall ('The most physical winger I ever played against'). He says:

> Although it was a physical game then, I was nowhere near close to being sent off, I don't think. I did not make those kind of tackles. More often than not, there was no physical contact at all because of my pace: I could sort of 'steal' the ball, lure people into taking an extra touch and nick the ball off them.
>
> I don't care who you are, there isn't one game in which the other team are not going to have a good spell. It might only be for ten or 15 minutes, but that's the time you've got to dig in. Don Revie used to say: 'If on top, you've sometimes got to battle to make sure you stay on top. If you don't and the other team seizes the initiative, it's very hard to gain control again.' It was important to me to be in charge of the player I was marking for the whole game, to sort of get it across to him that it was my game. I didn't like getting beaten. Instead of 40,000 people clapping the other guy because he had got past me, I wanted them to be clapping me. There was a bit of insecurity in it, I suppose – the feeling that if I didn't dominate the players I was marking, then the manager would soon have me out of the side and get someone who could.

There was only one occasion when Reaney can recall allowing himself to adopt a more liberal attitude. 'That was when he played for England against Scotland in an Under-23 international, and was faced with the dilemma of going into a crunching challenge on his Leeds colleague Billy Bremner. 'There was a fifty-fifty ball in midfield between Billy and myself; we both started going flat out for it and then, when we were maybe two or three yards from each other, we both just stopped and neither of us got it. We just smiled at one another.' It was unique cameo because, as Reaney says: 'I was very quiet on the field. Believe it or not, George and I never spoke when we were playing against each other, and that's the way I preferred it to be with everybody. I didn't want anyone talking to me – I didn't like people being nice to me, because I thought it might put me off doing what I had to do. For 90 minutes, you had to try and think: "I don't like you . . . I don't like you . . . I don't like you." If I had to dig in a little bit, I didn't want the other guy saying: "What did you do that for?" Remember Ian Storey-Moore, the former Nottingham Forest, Manchester United and England winger? He was a nice lad and it was so difficult to be physical with Ian because he'd tell you: "Oh Paul, that wasn't nice." Same with George Armstrong at Arsenal. It's hard, isn't it? It really is.'

Reaney, who was born in London but started living in Leeds when he was barely two weeks old, made a total of 743 first-team appearances in his 17 years at Leeds, a total bettered only by Jack Charlton. At the same time, among a famous all-international back four which included Hunter and Terry Cooper, he was arguably the one who attracted the least publicity. Certainly he did not catch the eye as much as Cooper on the other flank – none of his fellow defenders did. The sight of Charlton galloping the field to add his weight to the Leeds attack was perhaps the next best sight to behold, although when Leeds had truly got the creative bit between the teeth, even a man as determined to express himself as Charlton was made to feel like an unwanted guest at a party. In that respect Reaney reminds you of that famous 7–0 victory over Southampton in 1972, when Leeds mesmerised the Saints with a move involving some 27 passes, and the frustrated Charlton ran around with his arms in the air in his unsuccessful attempt to get in on the act. Cooper would have been the first to be invited to that sort of party, and Reaney perhaps the last.

After all, while Reaney was at his best when defending, Cooper – who could occasionally show even Best a thing or two in terms of going past opponents with the ball – was noted more for his attacking skills. Cooper, indeed, had been an outside left when joining Leeds in May 1961. Reaney, who arrived at Elland Road five months later, was a centre-half. 'I think the thing that most troubled Don Revie about me in that position was my height [5ft 10in]. He thought that, with my pace and mobility, I would be more effective out wide, and he was right. Not long after he switched me to right-back my father went down to Elland Road and said to him: "My son is a centre-half, he's not a full-back." Don said something like: "Well, you wait and see, just give me a month." The next time my dad went down, he had to say sorry.'

Reaney was not as much of a 'natural' footballer as Cooper. 'I had skill, but I had a lot to thank coaches like Syd Owen and Les Cocker for. They really worked on me and I worked hard on myself. My left foot wasn't as good as my right, although I did play for England once at left-back and I had to learn how to get the maximum out of myself when competing with fellows bigger than me in the air. I had a knack of dealing with this – I won't tell you what it was, but whereas I didn't used to win the ball, they didn't either. Just let's say that it was one of those tricks of the trade that you acquire and develop to get the best out of yourself. With me, it was just a question of learning, learning, learning and keeping your feet on the ground. The players you played made sure you did that anyway. If you did something wrong, or became a bit lazy, it wasn't so much the manager and the coaches who would give you stick, it was the other players.'

Reaney did have his adventurous attacking moments, but was less liable to turn himself into a hero in the way that Cooper did in the 1968 League Cup final against Arsenal. Today, most avid Leeds fans might be able to tell you that Cooper was so badly affected by nerves on the eve of the game that, after a restless night, he rose at 8 a.m. on the Saturday morning and while most of the others were still in bed, spent an hour jogging around the lawn adjoining the team's hotel and doing loosening-up exercises. They would certainly be able to tell you about what happened in the 20th minute of the game – the Bremner free-kick lofted into the Arsenal goalmouth; the challenge by Charlton and Paul Madeley on the Gunners' keeper, Jim Furnell, which led to the ball breaking loose to the edge of the box; and, of course, Cooper's ferocious first-time shot that brought the only goal of the game and Leeds's first major trophy.

He only got ten goals in all for Leeds, in 350 appearances, but those dazzling forward runs of his created countless goals for others. Hence the fact that, although Reaney ended up with only two fewer, Cooper's image among the fans was more charismatic. 'I do remember scoring the only goal at Coventry [to give Leeds the win they needed to keep in the Championship race in April 1972]. Norman Hunter told me: "It's amazing Paul – when I rung Sue [his wife] and asked her to name the player who scored for us, she went through every player except you." I used to get stick from the lads over my scoring record – not very often, to be fair, but Chris Lawler [the Liverpool full-back] scored so many goals it was untrue, and they'd occasionally say to me: "Why can't you do that?" Yet when I did go forward, and the move broke down, it was: "Hey – what are you doing up here? Get back." ' He laughs, and adds: 'I didn't create or score many goals, but how many I stopped was another aspect of it.'

Indeed, in addition to his ability to stifle wingers, and prevent them getting in dangerous crosses, Reaney was also noted for the high number of shots and headers he stopped on the goal-line. It was a part of his game, he says, which was acquired almost by chance. 'We had a flat back four and we used to play on a sort of swivel,' he explains. 'If the ball was on Terry's side, then I would move slightly inside and be the last man – there would be Terry, then Norman a little deeper, then Jack a little deeper and finally myself. If the ball was then transferred to my left winger, Terry would be the one to take up the covering position and I would have to get to my man. The goal-line clearances stemmed from that because, if the player was going to take a shot from say 20 yards, and I was maybe 15 yards from him and five yards from the goal-line, I thought: "Well, it will be quicker for you to position yourself on the line than to get to him." It's amazing how many times this worked for me. Gary Sprake [the Leeds goalkeeper] would cover three-quarters of the ball and I would cover the other quarter.'

It worked perfectly in the 1972 FA Cup final win against against Arsenal, when Reaney blocked a Ball shot on the line, with the score at 0–0. Two days later, however, with Leeds needing a point at Wolves to clinch the Championship-Cup double, it didn't. Wolves' first goal in their 2–1 win, an angled drive from Francis Munro three minutes before half time, was the most agonising of Reaney's career. Dave Harvey was in goal for Leeds then, and Reaney, referring to his understanding with Sprake, says: 'If he [Sprake] had been in goal, I think I would have stopped the shot. I was on the line, and I wasn't expecting Dave to come because the ball was heading straight towards me. But Dave dived right across me. He did well to get a hand to the ball, but he sort of touched it in.'

There were other low points for him, off the field as well as on it. In 1992, for example, he had all his medals stolen. 'We were over at our place in Spain for a while, and when we got back, we'd been burgled. My trophies and England caps weren't touched but we had a little safe then and I put the medals in it before we went on holiday. They actually took the safe. I'm still sad about it – I can't show the medals to my grandchildren. But what can you do about it?' There wasn't much he could have done either about the broken right leg he suffered in a league match at West Ham in a 2–2 draw on 2 April 1970, an injury which caused him to miss the Leeds-Chelsea FA Cup final, the second leg of the European Cup semi-final against Celtic and playing for England in the World Cup finals in Mexico.

This wasn't a good time for either Leeds full-back. Just 24 hours before the West Ham match, Leeds had lost 1–0 to Celtic in the European Cup semi-final first leg at Parkhead, their eighth fixture in 22 days. The only goal came in the first minute, when a moment of indecision by Reaney and Cooper as they chased a long ball down the left led to Wallace gaining possession and Connelly scoring from his cross. In the second leg at home, which Leeds lost 2–1, Cooper suffered a rare nightmare for 90 minutes against Jimmy Johnstone, not to mention Celtic's right-back, David Hay, who came forward down the flank so often that it seemed as if Celtic were playing with two wingers.

Still, Cooper would hardly have swapped his "pain" for Reaney's. I, too, have good cause to remember that match at West Ham. I'd attended the game as one of Revie's guests, and we had intended to have dinner together later at the team's hotel. On our arrival back there, Revie telephoned the hospital from the hotel foyer to ascertain the extent of Reaney's injury. The news hurt him as much as it did Reaney. The manager burst into tears and was inconsolable. Reaney recalls: 'It was one of those silly games where there was nothing at stake for either side [Leeds had conceded the Championship] and not much physical stuff. It was the first bad injury I'd had but, at 26, it was all there for me. I was at my peak. I had reached a stage in my career when the game was no effort – you know, you can play every day and you don't get tired.

'Norman Hunter and I had been in the England squad a long time before getting a kick. Norman couldn't get into the team because of Bobby Moore, and I couldn't get in because of George Cohen. I was chosen for the preliminary squad of 40 for the 1966 World Cup finals but was left out when it was reduced to 28. For the next one, there's me in, and I get a broken leg. What made it so agonising for me was that while the left-back position in the team was settled – we knew Terry Cooper would be filling it – the right-back one wasn't. So it was all there for me.'

But it was his position at Leeds that inevitably caused him the most anguish. 'Don couldn't tell me what was going to happen to me there – who knew what was going to happen? I was out for five or six months, and during that time you are worrying about not being able to turn as quick as you did before, or jump as high, things like that. Also Paul Madeley had slotted in well at right-back, and remember, you are not talking about an average player, you are talking about an England international, and you're thinking: "I'm going to have to get him out." Not easy.'

Reaney made his first-team return at West Bromwich Albion (2–2) in October 1970, played the next match at home to Manchester United (2–2) but did not play again until coming on as a substitute against Liverpool at Anfield (1–1) on 5 December. 'I thought I was doing it, but Don Revie didn't think I was. "You are not quite there yet," he said. So I was in and out of the side, and I didn't want to be in and out.' Reaney asked for a transfer and Leeds, reluctantly agreeing to it, then arranged to sell him for £100,000 – ironically to Manchester United. But Reaney suddenly turned the clock back to what he had been like before his injury, which prompted Revie to increase his selling price for the player to £150,000; he regained his regular first-team place and went on to give the club another eight years' sterling service. In so doing he emphasised the importance of teams having the right blend of players, of teams having players who could carry the piano as well as those who could play it. It is partly for this reason that, in selecting my Leeds dream team, I have given preference to Reaney over Cooper and Charlton – not to mention Madeley, the most versatile player in Britain. With the exception of Charlton, Reaney was arguably the member of the great Leeds team who had to work the hardest on his game, the one who came the closest to being looked upon as a 'manufactured' player. The same could be said of Madeley, whose fitness, strength and mobility saw him fill every position for Leeds except that of goalkeeper. It says much about Madeley's remarkable flexibility that, though not considered as an automatic member of their starting line-up when Leeds were at their peak, he still made 712 full appearances, just 24 short of Reaney's total, in his 17 years with the club.

However, no player did his job more diligently than Reaney. Such was the level of concentration Reaney reached to keep

Leeds solid at the back that he can remember little about any of the games in which he played. 'People ask me to single out my greatest game, but it's difficult. Remember, you are talking about 750 games here. I'd go home after some matches and think: "Oh, that was really brilliant," but you were too wrapped up in them to be able to really savour them. During a match, you weren't able to stand back and say: "Oh, look at that." The ball could be 60 yards away, on the other side of the field, but you still had to focus on what was happening and what might happen. That's where Don Revie was so good with his dossiers on opposing teams. You knew what the players you were marking were good at, what they weren't good at – you were thinking about these things and trying to read the game all the time.'

However, there are some games that stand out above the rest to him. One was his debut for Leeds, at 17, in the 2–0 win at Swansea in 1962. He remembers that when he told his parents he was in the side, they would not believe him. He also remembers the encouragement he received from the veteran Grenville Hair, the man he was replacing. 'Before I got on the team coach, he just said to me: "It's your turn now, son. I've had my turn." I thought that was super. Never forgotten that.'

Nor can he ever forget George Best, and the misery he inflicted upon him in those FA Cup semi-final ties against Manchester United in 1970. The one that really stood out was the first replay at Villa Park, which despite the 0–0 scoreline, has gone down as one of the most exciting matches ever seen at this stage of the competition. On that damp, gloomy March evening, the spectacle of two top-class teams going boldly for a win lit up the famous old stadium to the extent that Villa officials were left more crestfallen than ever about their own club's decline. The 62,500 who watched the game were as exhausted emotionally as those who played in it were physically. Villa had dropped into the Third Division that year, and one member of their staff said: 'We here had forgotten what football like this can be.'

United, whose line-up included not only Best, but also Bobby Charlton, Denis Law and Brian Kidd, had the edge in individual skill. Leeds's other handicap was that Hunter was out of the side because of injury. However, thanks to Reaney's stranglehold on Best – and that of Madeley doing a similarly good marking job on Charlton – it was Leeds who came the closest to scoring. In addition to some excellent Alex Stepney saves, Clarke had a 'goal' disallowed for a push on the keeper and also hit the bar.

For the replay at Burnden Park, Bolton, Revie, conscious of the fact that Reaney's role had disrupted Leeds's team 'shape', reverted to their usual zonal marking system. This, too, worked well. After ten minutes, Allan Clarke got his head to a Peter Lorimer chip, the ball cannoned off Mick Jones's legs, and Bremner blasted it past Stepney with his left foot. As for Reaney, he did not see as much of Best as he had done in the past. With Best being picked up by the Leeds defender who happened to be the nearest man to him, the likes of Cooper and Hunter were given the opportunity to test their ability against him.

One suspects that Best would have been happy to have been facing Bruce Lee or Clint Eastwood – anybody but the underrated Paul Reaney.

4

Don Revie

Don Revie was an emotional man, and on a damp, windy night at Anfield on Monday, 28 April 1969, he had much to get emotional about. That night, Leeds got the point they needed in their penultimate First Division match of the season – a goalless draw against Liverpool – to win the Championship for the first time in their history. As if that was not enough to bring a lump to the throats of Revie and everybody else connected with Leeds, the final whistle was followed by a moment that he was to describe as the most moving, and joyous, of his glittering managerial career. Norman Hunter recalls: 'In the dressing-room before the match, the gaffer turned to Billy and said: "Billy, if we win the title tonight, you and the lads will go over to the Kop." Our reaction was: "We can't do that, gaffer. How can we go over to the Kop?" We didn't think any more about it. Anyway, we've clinched the title, we're all jumping around on the pitch, and the gaffer goes to Billy: "Billy – the Kop." None of us wanted to do it, but the gaffer, he's adamant. So we make our way towards the Kop and as we get there, it's deathly quiet – deathly quiet. "I knew this was a mistake," I'm thinking. But then, suddenly, they started chanting: "Champions . . . Cham-pions" and the whole place just went whoosh – they gave us such a reaction, it was untrue. "Cham-pions . . . Cham-pions" I've never known anything like it. Just thinking about it now, I'm getting the old goose-bumps and the hair's standing on end.'

One can easily imagine how Revie must have felt. Just eight years earlier, when he had taken over as Leeds manager, the club had been striving to avoid relegation to the Third Division, let alone win the greatest prize in English football; and since their return to the First Division in 1964, the only trophies they had gained from four seasons of being at the forefront of the race for virtually all of them had been the League Cup and the European Fairs Cup. Indeed, they had suffered so many disappointments in the Championship – their earlier finishing positions had been 2nd-2nd-4th-4th – that they were beginning to be perceived as perennial bridesmaids.

What helped make that 1969 triumph so special for Revie was that it was clinched on one of the grounds of the clubs, and the managers, for whom he had the greatest respect and admiration. Liverpool's irrepressible Bill Shankly was one of three Scottish managers that Revie had got close to (the others were Manchester United's Matt Busby and Celtic's Jock Stein). It was a closeness born not just of professional respect, but the fact that Revie's schoolteacher wife Elsie was a Scot, from a north of the border football family. Shankly, Busby and Stein were contemporaries of her father, John Duncan, a Scottish international wing-half or inside forward in the 1920s, and Revie's manager at Leicester City in the 1940s.

Revie and Shankly, who telephoned each other regularly, were great rivals as well as friends. Shankly had taken over at Liverpool just two years before Revie's arrival at Elland Road, and Liverpool, too, were in the Second Division then. The two clubs rose to prominence at roughly the same time, with Liverpool being the first to assert themselves by gaining promotion to the First Division in 1962, winning the Championship in 1964 and the FA Cup – at the expense of Leeds in the final – in 1965. Leeds, the younger of the two teams, 'froze' in that match. They had done superbly to get this far, in their first season back in Division One, but Revie was so disappointed about their performance that in the Wembley dressing-room after the match, he told his team: 'You shouldn't be allowed to walk on this turf, let alone play on it.' It was an uncharacteristic outburst by Revie, and one he instantly regretted. However, this merely added more sweetness to that moment when the fans on the Kop acknowledged that Leeds could play for high stakes, and succeed – anywhere.

The manner in which Leeds clinched that point might have been more pragmatic than Revie would have wished. Nonetheless, there was nothing pragmatic about their overall record as one of the greatest Championship-winners of all time. That Leeds team amassed a record number of 67 points, one more than the previous best total set by Arsenal in 1931 and Tottenham in 1961. They also established a Championship record of only two defeats in 42 matches. Arsenal previously held that record with four defeats in 1931.

It is often said that, in order to fully appreciate triumphs like this, one has to experience the agony of the other side of the coin. Certainly Revie – who described his first 18 months as Leeds manager as his '18 months of hell' – went through more agony than anyone.

Born in Middlesbrough, the former Leicester, Hull, Manchester City, Sunderland and England inside forward was appointed Leeds player-manager in March 1961, at 34, following the resignation of Jack Taylor. He only had another season and a half to go on his contract as a Leeds player, and the then chairman, Harry Reynolds, recalled: 'Don was interested in the player-manager's job at Bournemouth and asked me to write a reference for him. As I was doing it, it suddenly occurred to me that we could do with him ourselves. So I just tore up the reference and offered him the post.' Revie, initially paid a basic salary of £1,900 a year, could hardly have viewed this as Reynolds doing him a favour. He told the beleaguered Leeds board: 'If we get back into the First Division in five years, we will have done exceptionally well.'

During those first 18 months, the quality of the playing staff he inherited from his predecessor Jack Taylor was so low that although he released as many as 18 players, the transfer fees for them totalled no more than £20,000. 'There were numerous occasions during that period when I'd tell Elsie that I'd had enough, there was no point carrying on. I found it very difficult to sleep – more often that not, I'd be up half the night, sitting in our lounge drinking pots of tea.'

However, Taylor did leave Revie one valuable legacy – two excellent backroom staff members in coach Syd Owen and trainer Les Cocker, both of whom had been enlisted in June 1960. Another valuable legacy was the advice of Matt Busby. When Revie went to see the Manchester United boss for advice on the job, Busby, renowned for the Old Trafford youth policy that produced the 'Busby Babes', inevitably stressed the importance of Leeds following United's lead. So Revie persuaded the Leeds board to bring back Maurice Lindlay, who had been sacked by the club as first-team coach just six months earlier, as chief scout. 'As a Leeds player, I had been impressed by Maurice's knowledge of the game and his handling of people,' Revie said. 'Unfortunately, the board made him the scapegoat for the club's lack of success. There was a stony silence when I told them I wanted him back, but I was determined to do the job my way, or not at all.'

Lindlay played a big part in the reorganisation and strengthening of Leeds's youth system, while Owen and Cocker helped Revie instil a greater sense of discipline and commitment into his senior squad. One way in which this was achieved was to force the Leeds board to dig deeper into their pockets to improve the players' Elland Road lifestyle. 'Although the club was heavily in debt, I insisted upon the players getting the same sort of star treatment as those at clubs like Manchester United and Tottenham,' Revie said. 'Everything about Leeds then was second class, from the balls we used in training to our hotels for away games. I just felt that we had to start thinking big, and that the lead had to come from the top.'

Some senior players reacted to this better than others. However, after a while, Revie's boundless energy and enthusiasm inevitably began to spread throughout the club. It was that energy and enthusiasm that enabled him to sign Bobby Collins from Everton in March 1962, when Leeds were struggling in the Second Division, and Collins, though in his thirties, was intent on not lowering his standards. Just to listen to Revie on the background to his signing of Collins was enough to make you feel weary: 'A journalist tipped me off that Everton might be willing to let Bobby go, so after we got confirmation of this from their manager, Harry Catterick, I travelled to Goodison the following morning, with two of our directors, to open negotiations. I spent an hour with Bobby after training, and he told me in no uncertain terms that he felt he still had a lot to offer as a First Division player, and didn't fancy the idea of going to a club with one foot in the Third. We left it that he would think it over for a couple of days, and get back to me. But as we headed for home, I decided to have another chat with him. I remember, we arrived at his house at 2 p.m. and waited in the car no less than five hours before he turned up. We didn't leave until 2.30 a.m. the next morning, but by that time, Bobby had agreed to join us. Even after the deal had been completed, Bobby continued to have doubts about it. In fact, just a few weeks later, he actually asked for a transfer.' That Revie was able to get him to change his mind again led to Leeds escaping relegation – and going from strength to strength.

However, while the acquisition of Collins proved the major turning point for Revie and Leeds, it was his determination to develop players of that calibre through the Elland Road youth system that yielded the most stunning dividends.

Quite apart from the ability of the numerous players turned out by that system, one could not help but admire their sense of unity. Leeds United were like a big, closely-knit family with

Revie, having been something of a guardian to many of them as boys, playing the part of its proud titular head. It would be difficult to imagine any manager inspiring greater loyalty and respect from his troops than Revie did. His concern about their welfare was epitomised during the early part of his Leeds career, when one senior player fell into financial difficulty and needed £500 to stave off the threat of his business being declared bankrupt. Revie promised the player that the board would loan him the money, but the directors refused. So Revie, with only £750 in his own bank account at the time, lent it to him himself. The other example of Revie's determination to support his players was provided by their Welsh international goalkeeper, Gary Sprake, a brilliant natural keeper but a player who lived on his nerves on the big occasion and who was prone to glaring mistakes. Sprake, indeed, could be unreliable off the field as well as on it, yet Revie stuck by him more firmly than many deemed advisable.

In truth, though Revie was labelled a greedy opportunist when he walked out on the England job to become football supremo of the United Arab Emirates, those close to him paint a rather different picture of the man. To those he cared about, and especially those who had helped him during his career, his spirit of generosity could hardly be faulted. He felt deeply about his wife Elsie's family, and especially her mother, three of her aunts and an uncle, all of whom were persuaded by Revie to leave their home in Scotland and live with him and Elsie in Leeds so they could take care of them in their old age. Revie once confided: 'These marvellous old people [all in their seventies and eighties at the time] have been great to us. They all helped bring Elsie up after she lost her father when she was a small girl, and they did a lot for us when we got married.'

His attitude to his players was little different. Jim Storrie, one of his earliest signings – from Airdrie in 1962 – recalled: 'I scored quite a few goals in my first season with Leeds, but hit a bad patch the next season. The harder I tried to get out of it, the worse it became. But Don called me into his office and said he appreciated what I was going through and would support me to the hilt. He said: "Get your wife and kids up to Scotland for a two-week holiday. You can do anything you like, as long as you take a complete break from football." When I came back, I would do anything for him. He was never too busy to spend a few minutes asking you how your family were. Most managers do it out of politeness, but with Don, you felt he was really interested. One day, I happened to mention that my son wasn't well, so he immediately arranged for the club doctor to give him a thorough check-up. All this might seem trivial to outsiders, but you'd be surprised how much these things can help to establish a good team spirit and player-manager relationships.' Revie put it this way: 'I was unhappy as a player because I felt that many managers had little interest in the men under their command. I was determined that, if I moved into the managerial chair, things would be different.'

Not that Revie was a soft touch. Indeed, Revie's Leeds United 'sons' – as with all sons when they step out of line – were all somewhat wary of upsetting him.

All the Leeds players vividly recall an incident that occurred during Leeds's trip to Italy for the European Fairs Cup final first leg in May 1971. Revie had decided to take the players' wives and girlfriends so they could spend some time with them after the game; and though the match was abandoned after 51 minutes because of a waterlogged pitch, he saw no reason why the arrangement should be changed. Thus, while Revie was locked in discussions over the replay date, the players were allowed to go to the Turin hotel where their nearest and dearest were staying so they could have dinner together. In the meantime, Revie arranged for the Leeds team to remain in Turin and play the tie again on the Friday – and for the womenfolk to remain there, too, at the club's expense. However, when Revie caught up with the party late on Wednesday night, four of the players did not want to return to their hotel. 'We want to stay here with our wives,' one insisted. In the row that followed, Revie told them: 'If that's your attitude, I am going home tomorrow and you can find yourself a new manager.' Shortly afterwards, however, Revie, in another part of the hotel, was given the message that all the players were on the team coach, ready to leave. When Revie himself got there, he found the wives lined up on the hotel forecourt, each looking decidedly sheepish and saying: 'Sorry, Mr Revie,' as he walked past.

Peter Lorimer says: 'If you produced a below-par performance, he wouldn't say anything to you immediately after the match – I think he learned from one or two incidents early in his career at Leeds that it was best to wait until the Monday morning, when everyone had cooled down. But you could tell that he had the raving needle, and the best thing that you could do was keep your head down and not say a word to him. I remember, he'd come into the dressing-room, his face as black as thunder. He was obviously going to go into the boardroom, because he'd just go over to the mirror, sort of tidy his hair, and walk straight out, slamming the door behind him. Until he left, there'd be absolute silence in that dressing-room; you could cut the atmosphere with a knife.' Even Billy Bremner, Revie's captain and arguably the Leeds player towards whom Revie adopted the most liberal attitude, occasionally had cause to fear that he might have pushed him too far. 'He was a big man,' Bremner recalls, 'and when he banged those big fists of his on the table . . .' Bremner shakes his head and adds: 'He looked after the boys ever so well – perhaps too well. In my own case, he wanted me to achieve success and the rewards that went with it, as much as I wanted it myself, probably even more. I always remember the rollickings he gave me when I came back to Leeds after playing for Scotland. He felt that I was worrying too much about helping other players and not enough about my own game. He said: "You're covering up for this player, you're covering up for that player – you should be doing more to express yourself." My argument was that this was the way I was, and it was the way he had brought me up to play at Leeds. "Yeah," he'd say, "but at international level, a lot of players play for themselves. They would never bother their backsides about you, Bill." All the time, you knew that he was looking after your interests, you know?'

It has been said that Revie took this to the extreme, that he was too 'possessive' with his players, both as people and footballers. He once described himself as a 'born worrier', a characteristic that could make him appear almost neurotic. Strange as it might seem, Bremner insists that Revie did not coach his players anywhere near as much as many outsiders believe. Nonetheless, his influence on them in other ways – on their mentalities and approach to the game – was exceptionally powerful. To an extent, his methods mirrored a strong streak of insecurity in him, as highlighted by his exhaustive, in-depth dossiers on the strengths and weaknesses of opposing teams, his unwillingness to leave anything to chance in his preparation for matches, and his deeply superstitious nature.

Terry Yorath, who as a Leeds substitute often sat beside Revie in the touchline dug-out, once said: 'During one game, he turned to me and said: "The lads look uptight today, don't they?" I thought: "Well, looking at how uptight you seem, it's little wonder." ' Bremner, too, gives an insight into this side of Revie when he says: 'We didn't just have a great team under him, we had a great squad – a group of 16 or 17 players who were all internationals and who would all have walked into the first teams of most other clubs. But he had this thing about playing the same 11 all the time, no matter what. There were loads of times when you would be struggling with an injury – not just me, all the guys – but he'd say: "Oh, you on one leg is better than what I've got left." '

All this led to the thought that Revie's greatest strengths were also his biggest faults; that Leeds could not be relied upon to withstand the pressures of the last lap of a season and, indeed, that they did not win as much as they should have done. Certainly, in hindsight, it is not difficult to appreciate why he did not live up to expectations as England's manager, a post in which his long spells of being cut off from his players – his inability to mould them into his ways – caused that insecurity to become more pronounced than ever. Notwithstanding the argument that he probably did not have as many outstanding players to choose from as he had at Leeds, it was difficult, if not impossible, for him to create the same dressing-room 'chemistry'. At England level, the players, imbued with the different habits of their clubs, were more independent and less in awe of Revie than his Leeds men. Hence the fact that, while it was second nature to the Leeds players to stick together as a unit and spend the eve of matches involved in such 'bonding' pastimes as carpet bowls and bingo, a number of England stars scoffed at this.

Revie, therefore, became more and more frustrated – and disillusioned. However, the one thing he never lost was his humility. Looking back on his Leeds career, he kept saying how lucky he was to have gathered so many great players around him at the same time. Moreover, on the question of the number of trophies that slipped through Leeds's grasp, especially in the early years, he admitted: 'Don't blame the players, blame me. I kept our players tied to a rigid tactical system for too long. It makes me feel sick when I think of the number of times we deployed the likes of Billy Bremner and John Giles in defensive roles. In some ways, I think it was the right thing to do in our first couple of seasons in the First Division. The lads were inexperienced at this level, so for me, we needed a "tight" system of play which would ensure reasonably good results and enable the lads to consolidate their status. But I should have taken them off the leash and let them express their creative ability earlier than I did.'

Bremner, though, echoes the view of all his Leeds players when he insists that Revie was being much too hard on himself. The other salient point, of course, is that when Revie did start to relax, and allow the creative element of his side to blossom, the football Leeds played made it well worth the wait.

It was in that 1968/69 season that Revie took the first conscious step towards this. The previous season, when Leeds finished fourth, Revie noted that the main difference between them and the champions, Manchester City, was that City gained more away wins. 'We ourselves tended to be too cautious away from home, and settle for draws in situations where we should have aimed for victory.' So Revie made up his mind that his team would be more positive, although when he called the players together for a campaign briefing during the close season, he gave them a target of a different and altogether more demanding kind. 'You are going to win the title this season,' he said, 'and what's more, you are going to do it without losing a single league match.'

They were helped by the fact that they were beaten at early stages of the FA Cup and League Cup, and the fourth round of the Fairs Cup, and were able to focus on the Championship more closely than in previous seasons. As for Revie's demand for more wins away from home, Leeds set themselves the right example before the start of the season with a 2–1 win over Celtic, the Scottish champions, in a friendly match watched by a Hampden Park crowd of 75,000. Over the next seven days, Leeds also beat Hungary's Ferencvaros 1–0 in the European Fairs Cup final (held over from the previous season), and kicked off their First Division programme with a resounding 3–1 win at Southampton. Leeds then gained five wins and two draws in their next seven matches and the eighth, a 2–0 home win over Arsenal, took them to the top of the table.

If there was one match during this period that summed up the resolve and concentration of this remarkable Leeds team it was at Nottingham Forest, where the game was abandoned at half-time because of a fire in the main stand. Bremner recalls that the players were listening so intently to Revie's instructions for the second half that they were completely oblivious to the wisps of smoke billowing through the dressing-room door. When Sprake attempted to draw Bremner's attention to it, he was told: 'Shut up, Gary, the gaffer is talking.'

It was in their ninth match that Leeds suffered their first League defeat of the season, 3–1 at Manchester City. After taking maximum points from their next three games, they faltered again by losing to Crystal Palace in the League Cup and, more alarmingly, 5–1 at Burnley in the League on 19 October. But that was the end of their bad spell. They were unbeaten in their remaining 28 matches, winning 17 of them and conceding only 11 goals in all. In view of the fierce pride running through the team, it will have come as no surprise that the most emphatic of those victories was a 5–1 thrashing of Burnley at home, in December.

By the end of March, Leeds held a five-point lead over Liverpool, their closest rivals, who had played one match fewer and who had yet to face Leeds at home. In the first of their remaining eight fixtures, Leeds drew 0–0 at Sheffield Wednesday, beat Manchester City 1–0 at home and then had another draw (after being behind) at West Bromwich Albion. Three days later, Leeds had what Bremner described as their best win of the season, 2–1 at Arsenal.

The Gunners had sensationally lost to Swindon in the League Cup final the previous month, but were unbeaten at home. 'It was generally felt we would do well to get a point,' Bremner recalls, 'and we would have been happy to settle for that result because a win would have blasted the Championship race wide open.' Leeds nearly came unstuck as early as the fourth minute, when Sprake clashed with the Gunners' combative centre-forward Bobby Gould, and landed a short left hook on Gould's chin. Fortunately for Leeds, the referee, Ken Burns, who could easily have sent off Sprake, was content to just give him and Gould a lecture. It was from that point that the perceptiveness of Revie and his players in pinpointing and exploiting the opposition's vulnerable spots came into play. Revie had noted that Arsenal's central defender, Frank McLintock, tended to come too far forward and didn't give his partner, Ian Ure, enough cover. So it was no coincidence that when Leeds broke up an Arsenal attack deep in their own half, Mick Bates pumped a high clearance down the middle, and it was no surprise that, when Ure misjudged the flight of the ball, Mick Jones had a clear run on goal. Revie also noted that Ure, not the best of ball-players, could be pressurised into loose passes. That, too, was brought into sharp focus when Leeds, having conceded a George Graham equaliser, got the winner from Giles as a result of the midfielder forcing Ure into a wayward back pass.

Leeds maintained their five-point lead by beating Leicester at home the following Saturday and drawing 0–0 at Everton three days later. They had 64 points from 40 matches, while Liverpool had 59 points from 39 games. So the crunch match at Anfield was Liverpool's last opportunity to keep their Championship hopes alive, and a golden chance for Leeds to bring theirs to fruition. A golden chance for the team Revie had built to emphasise his faith in them.

On the eve of the game, even the normally devil-may-care Bremner experienced an attack of nerves. 'I couldn't sleep the night before, which was very unusual for me,' he says. 'I even got out of bed at four in the morning to have a cigarette and try to stop thinking about the game. I think all the lads felt the same way. When they went out, they were more uptight than I had ever known them to be before. I think we felt the tension even more than we did in the FA Cup final [against Liverpool in 1965].'

This, indeed, was a match to fully test Leeds's temperament rather than their skill. As expected, Liverpool pushed Leeds back on the defensive for most of the game, and had the clearest scoring chances. Both fell to Alun Evans, the young Liverpool centre-forward who on each occasion had only Sprake to beat, but the first he fired over from six yards, and then miscued a shot from a similarly good position. Sprake himself made the save of the match, from Ian Callaghan. How Liverpool missed the experience and composure of their injured England striker Roger Hunt. However, it was significant that Liverpool had to stretch themselves to the limit to create such opportunities and that their attacking play lacked its usual fluency. As a result of their failure to get an early goal, they became over-anxious and fell into the trap of hitting high balls into the Leeds goalmouth, where Evans and Bobby Graham up front were no match for Sprake and Jack Charlton in the air.

The more pressure that Liverpool put on Leeds, the stronger Leeds seemed to become. Bremner recalls: 'I could not see Leeds scoring, but the way the game was going, I honestly couldn't see Liverpool scoring either. The conditions were difficult – a windy night, hard bumpy pitch – and Liverpool's midfield players couldn't build up anything worth while because the ball was going back and forth over their heads. Mind you, we only played for an hour and a half, but to me, the match seemed to last five hours.' The Leeds fans clearly had that impression, too: with the last minutes ticking away, and Liverpool making their last desperate push for victory, their howls for the referee to blow the final whistle reached almost hysterical proportions.

And then, this titanic duel was over, leaving those who had witnessed it in a daze of either happiness or despair. 'Champions . . . Cham-pions . . . Cham-pions,' chanted the Kop choir in salute of perhaps the only team on earth who could have stood as firm against them as Leeds had done.

It sounded so good to everyone connected with Leeds, but particularly to Don Revie.

5

Eddie Gray

Before England faced Scotland at Wembley in Euro 96, Eddie Gray MBE took part in an exhibition curtain-raiser between teams made up of former internationals from the two countries. In both his appearance and his impact on the game, the 48-year-old coach of Leeds United's youth team belied the fact that he was the oldest player on the field. He looked little different to the Gray whose exquisite ball-playing skills had once made him one of the best outside lefts seen in Britain since the war, a winger in the same category as even Stan Matthews and Tom Finney, Jimmy Johnstone and George Best. But as Gray gave us glimpses of his mastery of the ball that day, making football at this level look ridiculously easy, and helped his team win 3–1, he was struck by a feeling of regret – even resentment. 'I was thinking about the wonderful condition of the Wembley pitch,' he explains. 'It was the best I had ever seen it. I was thinking: "They've obviously not staged the Horse of the Year show on it this year"!'

The trace of sarcasm in that remark, uncharacteristic for a man renowned as one of the game's gentlemen, was nonetheless understandable. The last occasion Wembley staged the Horse of the Year Show, in fact, was in 1970, just before the Leeds–Chelsea FA Cup final in which Gray gave one of the most enthralling individual displays ever seen at this English football mecca. Today that match is remembered as the 'Gray Final', for the same reason that the 1953 Blackpool–Bolton final is remembered as the 'Matthews Final'. Many feel that even Matthews did not excite the audience quite like Gray did, especially as those watching Gray will have been left in no doubt that, instead of being helped by the Wembley conditions – as one would have expected any top-class player to be – he was handicapped by them.

The description of the Wembley pitch as a lush green carpet had become inappropriate some time before Gray stepped on to it in 1970. But, through a combination of the wet weather and the damage caused by those galloping horses' hooves, it was rendered so bare and uneven that some 100 tons of sand had to be poured on it. Indeed, the pitch was so unrecognisable as the surface one would normally have expected to find at Wembley that Leeds, mindful of the psychological effect that such problems can have on players, decided against taking the team to Wembley for the traditional eve-of-the-final walk on the pitch. Instead, the players had a light work-out in a park close to their hotel. 'We are not proud of the pitch,' a Wembley spokesman was reported as saying, 'but it is playable. Let it go at that.'

However, this inevitably proved difficult in the case of Leeds, the more skilful of the two teams and therefore the one for whom the surface created the biggest headaches. Though both teams managed to overcome the conditions well enough to provide one of the most entertaining finals since the war, it was difficult to avoid the view that Leeds – held to a 2–2 draw after extra-time, after twice being in front – would have won reasonably comfortably had the stage on which Gray wove his magic and set up so many of their chances been firmer and more consistent. 'I never realised how much we were on top in that game until I recently watched it again on TV,' Gray says. 'Obviously, I knew we were the better team while I was playing in the game, but watching it in the cold light of day years later is a real eye-opener in terms of the number of chances we created. Had it been a normal game, we would probably have won by six.'

The failure to take advantage of those chances had sad repercussions for Gray, and Leeds. Chelsea, boosted by the feeling that they were fated to emerge victorious, and fielding a team better suited to stopping Gray, again fought back from behind to beat them 2–1 in the replay at Old Trafford. It was the last, cruel blow in a season of bitter disappointment for Leeds, who had put themselves in a good position to achieve the unprecedented treble of the Championship, European Cup and FA Cup . . . but ended up with nothing.

One would needed to have been a sadist not to feel sorry for Leeds. Before their First Division match at home to Southampton on 28 March 1970, they had played a total of 52 competitive matches, and lost only three – to Everton and Newcastle in the League, and Chelsea in the League Cup. But in the next 33 dismal days, a high-pressure finale to the season which saw them virtually buried under an avalanche of matches, they won only one in ten. It is significant that immediately before the Southampton match, they had been involved in three particularly gruelling FA Cup semi-final battles with Manchester United, eventually winning through 1–0 after two goalless draws. At this point, Leeds decided that, of the three trophies they had been chasing the Championship was the one furthest from their reach; and that leaving out key players for their First Division matches was the best way in which they could maximise their chances in the other two. On the face of it, the decision made perfect sense, but the Football League did not see it that way: they fined Leeds £5,000 for fielding 'weakened' teams. Moreover, as Revie later admitted: 'After our Cup ties against Manchester United, the club doctor had told me that the players were mentally and physically drained, but maybe I placed too much emphasis on this. They *were* tired, no doubt about that, but maybe the decision we made put this into their minds.'

Losing, like winning, can become a habit and Leeds quickly got into the habit of losing in the League, with defeats by Southampton and Derby over the Easter programme. Their remaining four First Division matches produced further defeats against Manchester City and Ipswich, a draw against West Ham and a sole victory over Burnley. More agonising, though, were the defeats they suffered in the semi-final of the European Cup (Celtic overcame them 1–0 at Elland Road and 2–1 at Parkhead) . . . and, of course, the FA Cup final.

Hard luck on Leeds, and extraordinarily hard luck on Gray, whose battle against the odds to produce such a memorable performance at Wembley extended beyond the problems posed by that pitch.

In addition to his creative talent – his balance, ball control, change of pace and accurate distribution – Gray was also noted for the high number of injury problems that dogged his career and, indeed, might easily have caused him to quit. True, Gray made more first-team appearances – 561 – than most other post-war Leeds players, but these were spread over 19 years. Moreover, Gray, whose playing career with Leeds stretched from January 1965 (when he joined the club as an apprentice at 16) to May 1984 (the culmination of two years as player-manager of the club), gained only 12 Scotland caps. His injury record made him an obvious target for Brian Clough's acerbic form of motivation when Clough succeeded Don Revie as Leeds manager. Clough, anxious to put his own stamp on the team – a process which involved his deliberately undermining and provoking them – told Gray: 'If you had been a racehorse, you would have been shot long ago.' Gray himself admits: 'I would say that I was never 100 per cent fit at any time in my career.'

The trouble started when Gray was just 16, and pulled a thigh muscle while playing in a reserve match against Sheffield Wednesday at Elland Road. He did more serious damage – a thigh muscle tear – through trying to come back too quickly, and put himself out of action for almost a year. 'Although I was playing for the team again at 17, the thigh bugged me all the way through my career, especially the important years of my career,' he says. 'The operations I had to undergo led to scar tissue, and with the development of scar tissue, the muscle gets shorter. So whenever I stretched the leg, I always used to have this pain. I could run, but I had to be careful when I was sprinting.' He certainly did not have the explosiveness of wingers such as Celtic's Jimmy Johnstone, a wizard of a player who captivated Gray not just with his dazzling dribbling skills but with his ability to suddenly spurt forward like a sprinter coming out of the blocks, then just as suddenly stop and put his foot on the ball, causing the man marking him to run past him. Gray, though, utilised his ball-playing skills in a more elegant, economical manner. 'I was still quick enough to get by people. I mean, John Robertson [the ex-Nottingham Forest and Scotland winger] wasn't lightning quick, but he knew when and how to use his pace. He had two great feet, and all he needed was half a yard. He'd get half a yard past someone and then – whoosh, that was the time for him to get the ball across. But it was still frustrating sometimes to know that, running-wise, I couldn't really let myself go. It was the same when it came to kicking the ball. I could never kick the ball how I really wanted to. I could never drive through it that much – I had to "cheat" a wee bit by sort of clipping it.'

However, just try relating all this to men such as David Webb, the Chelsea right-back facing Gray at Wembley, and the members of the Burnley defence who succumbed to a wonder goal by Gray in their 2–1 League defeat at Elland Road earlier that month. In the latter match, Gray, who had already scored the opener, dribbled through the Burnley defence with a repertoire of feints and tricks that could easily have landed him a first-team place with the Harlem Globetrotters. His delicate touch was also emphasised by his crosses and corners. In the latter case, one of Leeds's most effective ploys was to have big Jack Charlton standing on the goal-line, in front of the goalkeeper. As if this was not unsettling enough for a defence,

Gray could virtually drop the ball onto Charlton's head.

It was not just as an outside left that Gray was a top-class act. Having been originally signed by Leeds as a wing-half, the position he filled as one of the most sought after Scotland schoolboy internationals for years, he later played in almost every position or role except that of goalkeeper. Particularly beneficial to him was his experience towards the end of his career of operating at the back, as a sweeper or right or left full-back, areas which gave him more time to assess situations and imposed less of a physical strain on him:

> The older and more experienced I got, the more I learned how to avoid the danger of the thigh going again, without it detracting from my effectiveness. If you look at my career, you'll see that from the age of 26 or 27, I did not miss as many games as I did before that. I must be honest, there were times when I thought I'd never play again. I had five operations on the thigh between the ages of 16 and 24, and I think it must have frustrated the gaffer a lot that I was missing so many matches. Well, I know it did. It was a difficult situation for him. The thigh would be OK for a couple of weeks and then it would just go again. He could easily have said: 'Well, I never know if I can rely on you.' Funnily enough, one of the players in the England team for that match I played at Wembley [before the Euro 96 clash between the two countries] was Dave Thomas [the former Burnley winger]. I think there were times when the gaffer was thinking of signing him, which I don't think he would have done had I been 100 per cent fit.
>
> I was fortunate in that Leeds had such a big squad, full of internationals. A lot of the lads could play anywhere – that's the thing with great footballers, they can do a lot of different jobs – so anybody who was out of the team wasn't missed that much. But Don Revie was great for me, and at the end of the day I suppose it worked out well for both of us. From my point of view, it was just a question of accepting that I couldn't do what I wanted to do, and adjusting to it.

The mind boggles at the thought of what Gray would have been like had he been able to do so. The aspect of his game which characterised him the most was his ability to go past opponents as if they weren't there; the fact that he could beat them on either side, often just with a shake of his shoulders or hips. No doubt experts on the subject of balance and movement, like the famous Newcastle United guru Len Heppell, would single out Gray as the perfect example for their pupils to follow. In terms of being able to twist and turn suddenly, gain a yard or two on an opponent without losing his feet, Gray – his body hunched over the ball and with both arms out wide almost like those of a high-wire artist – had the ideal running gait. The position of his arms, he says, stemmed from a habit he had picked up when playing football in the street as a boy. 'The arms were held out for balance, but also to keep people off, without fouling them. At the school I went to in Glasgow, we used to play in a concrete yard, so you had to use your arms to prevent people knocking you over or into the wall.'

As a schoolboy, Gray's favourite team was Celtic, and his favourite player their left winger, Willie Fernie, who gained 12 Scotland caps – the same as himself – between 1954 and 1958. 'When I was playing for my school team at the ages of seven, eight, nine, people said I was greedy with the ball because I'd always be trying to take on people and was never put off by losing the ball. But I was influenced by watching Willie Fernie – he was like that. He'd lose the ball, and you'd think: "Oh, he should have passed it." But then he'd take people on again, he'd go past three or four of them, and it was a goal. That's how kids learn the game. I learned a lot from watching Bobby Collins at Celtic, too. You know, the way he could take three or four players out of the game just with a sway of the hips – incredible. Whether it's dribbling or passing or whatever, I learned what I wanted to do in the game from going to watch those players.'

Gray, in fact, has never lost his soft spot for Celtic. 'The Celtic result is still the first one I look for on a Saturday night,' he says. 'I had a fantastic career with Leeds, but if there was one thing I could say I regretted, it was that I didn't wear that green and white strip in a game at Celtic Park. It would have been nice to have that experience because my father was a big Celtic fan and he always wanted me to play for them.' Gray's brother, Frank, came closer to realising his father's ambition: he was a ball-boy at Celtic before following Eddie to Leeds, as a full-back. However, since Gray senior's death in 1972, one member of the family who has made it into the Celtic team is Eddie's son, Stuart, a midfield player. 'It's a pity my father wasn't alive to see it,' Gray says. 'He would have loved that. It has been wonderful for me, too. I've got to be honest, it's the thing that has given me the most satisfaction in all my time in football, watching Stuart play for Celtic against Rangers. It's something I will treasure for the rest of my life.' He has another son, ten-year-old Nicholas – ironically a Rangers supporter – who has been attending Leeds United's School of Excellence. 'He looks as if he is going to be a professional football player as well.'

However, all the young Grays – including Frank's son Andrew, a Leeds United first-team player – will be hard pressed to end their careers with the acclaim that Eddie attracted. One of the reasons for this was his temperament. He worked harder off the ball than other wingers, and was one of the bravest when it came to shrugging off opponents who tried to intimidate him physically (on the rare occasions that they were able to get close enough to him). In contrast to other members of a notoriously confrontational Leeds team, the mild-mannered Gray had an exemplary record. Not once was he sent off, or even booked. 'I like to win all the time,' he says. 'My wife, Linda, used to get annoyed with me when the kids were younger, because I didn't like them beating me at anything. But I was lucky in as much as I had the temperament to be able to walk away from things. If people kicked me, it didn't bother me. I thought: "Well, I've got them now." I used to laugh at some of the confrontations [concerning other Leeds players]. If the referee made a decision, then for me, that was it. You're never going to get him to change his mind. But Billy, John, Norman . . . they'd be chasing after him, shouting and complaining. It was great fun.

'When I was young, Don Revie said to me: "Always think of three c's: confidence, concentration and courage." He meant "courage" in the sense of character. For example, when I went to Rochdale as manager [in December 1986], the boys said to me: "It must have been easy playing in a team like Leeds." I said: "Yes, and no." The thing about it is that Leeds were under enormous pressure to keep winning, and you'd get matches at Elland Road where, if you weren't a goal or two ahead after 20 minutes, the crowd would start to have a go at you. I reminded them of what Don Revie had told me. That's when you need courage – you need it to keep playing.'

For all his natural ability, he feels he owes much to the early help he got from Leeds's coach, Syd Owen, the former Luton and England centre-half. 'Syd had me in tears at times, when I was 15, getting on to me all the time. He was a hard taskmaster and I think he got on some of the lads' nerves occasionally. But for me, he was a wonderful coach. He taught me a lot about the game, and how you should approach it. Initially, when I joined Leeds, I stayed with Syd for a few weeks, with Jimmy Lumsden [a fellow Glaswegian player at Leeds]. We'd be training at Elland Road all day, and then we'd go to Syd's place, and he would take us for a five-mile walk over the local golf course. Jim and I would be jiggered, but it taught us discipline and the importance of keeping in good shape. That's why I still train to this day; I still go regularly for five-, six-mile runs, and I love doing it.'

He was less enamoured about the position Leeds gave him – given the choice, he says he would have liked to play in midfield rather than out wide:

I was the same as John Giles, in that he was used to playing outside right when he came to the club – he'd never played midfield – and he did not enjoy it. But the difference was that, though I never considered myself to be a natural winger, I had a different type of ability to John so from that point of view, I was still able to get a lot of enjoyment from the role.

I have always been a great believer in people taking on defenders, not playing too much in front of them. As soon as you get past one defender, the whole game opens up. It's a different ball game you are playing then. But I wasn't just a dribbler, I could pass the ball as well, so it didn't bother me that much if I couldn't go past people with the ball. If that didn't work for me, I could also get by people with passing, hitting balls in behind them or playing one-twos.

One of the great things about it was that I could never come off the park saying that I didn't get good enough service. Well, I wouldn't have said it anyway, because you were brought up at Leeds not to look for excuses and Billy and John would have kicked you up the backside. But you could never say it because I did get the service most times. We had so many great players, and I had one of the best attacking left-backs in the world [Terry Cooper] behind me. He was great going forward, so with him bombing down the line, it took a lot of the attention off me. With the number of attacking outlets and options Leeds had, you could always create space to play in. I felt quite relaxed – there wasn't a team I didn't think we could beat. No matter who we were playing, I'd look at Jack [Charlton] and Norman [Hunter] and think: 'Phew, we're going to be hard to score against for a start.' Then you'd look at Billy and Johnny, Clarkey ... honestly, I can't remember one match where I thought we were going to get beaten. The players in that team had a tremendous knowledge of the game. Whatever the weak spots in the opposing team, our team would quickly find and exploit. This is where Johnny was so important. He would be the man who would suss it out straight away.

It certainly didn't take Giles, and the other Leeds players, long to suss out the advantages of repeatedly directing the ball to Gray in that 1970 FA Cup final against Chelsea. Gray was helped to a great extent by the manner in which Chelsea elected to reshuffle their attack in the absence of midfielder Alan Hudson. The most crucial aspect of this as far as Gray was concerned was that Tommy Baldwin, brought into the side at outside right, spent most of his time operating in the middle or on the other flank and therefore the man marking Gray, right-back Webb, was often forced to do so single-handedly. 'After a bit, the first ten or 15 minutes, I thought: "If we get enough of the ball out here, we could create a lot of chances," ' Gray recalls. 'Throughout the game, we were creating chances all over the park, but as for myself, the thing was that, once or twice, he [Webb] couldn't even get close enough to me to have a kick at me.' Webb, indeed, was given the biggest roasting of his career by Gray, in addition to the chances he created for others, twice came close to scoring himself with efforts that struck the bar. Here were some of the other highlights from his Wembley show:

21min. Curled in a corner for Charlton to head Leeds in front.

23min. Crossed to set up a chance for Lorimer, which was blocked on the line.

25min. Fastened on to a cross from the opposite flank to shoot narrowly wide.

30min. Drifted past two defenders and again was just off target with the shot.

42min. Beat three men this time, and flashed a low drive across the goal.

65min. Another dribble past three defenders, followed by a cross which two of his Leeds team-mates missed completely.

95min. Laid on a golden opportunity for Giles, only for Giles's effort to be cleared off the line.

Ironically, for all Leeds's polished football, it had taken a goal that owed more to luck than it did to skill to put them ahead. Charlton climbed well for Gray's corner, and got his header on target, but with two Chelsea players, Ron Harris and Eddie McCreadie, standing on the goal-line, a clearance looked a formality. McCreadie, though, was deceived by the bounce of the ball on that suet pudding pitch, and it squelched under his foot and into the net. The conditions also played a big part in Chelsea's equaliser, against the run of play, just before half-time – a low, speculative shot by Peter Houseman which, though Gary Sprake appeared to have well covered, slipped under the keeper's body. It was a bad moment, psychologically, for Leeds to concede a goal, but as Giles later said: 'We had been so much in command that I still couldn't see us not winning.' The bulk of the Wembley crowd will have seen little to cause them to think differently as Leeds continued to bombard the Chelsea goal in the second half.

Chelsea had their moments, too, especially when Sprake had to make a point-blank save from Ian Hutchinson and Hunter blocked Peter Osgood's follow-up effort on the line. During this period, however, Leeds were arguably more on top than at any other stage in the game. Certainly, it hardly came as a surprise when Leeds restored their lead seven minutes from the end. The move began with a flighted ball by Giles into the middle, where Clarke headed against an upright. But, just as we were thinking of it as another goal that had eluded Leeds, Mick Jones, for once free of the attentions of his marker, John Dempsey, was able to steady himself and dispel the gloom among Leeds fans with a left-foot shot into the left-hand corner of the net.

It was all over bar the shouting – or so it seemed. Three minutes later, Chelsea were level again, when Charlton conceded a free-kick for a foul on Peter Osgood. The Leeds defence were caught unprepared as Ron Harris, Chelsea's iron man captain, knocked the ball to John Hollins, and Hutchinson applied the finishing touch to Hollins's pass with a header by the near post. In truth, despite Charlton's claims that the free-kick should not have been awarded, it was a goal for which Leeds only had themselves to blame. 'We paid the price for lack of concentration,' Revie said, adding that he had been conscious of the danger of this when Leeds scored their second goal, but had been prevented by police from getting close enough to the pitch to warn his players. Bremner admitted: 'When we got that second goal, I was so excited, I couldn't think straight.' The analytical brain of Giles prompted the suggestion that Chelsea's goal could be attributed to Sprake's failure to prevent Chelsea taking the free-kick quickly. 'Gary tried to kick the ball into the crowd, but did not connect properly, and it went straight to Hollins of all people.' Not surprisingly in view of the amount of attacking Leeds had done, it was Chelsea who looked the fresher of the two teams in extra-time, with the match becoming more evenly contested as a result. However, even at the end of extra-time, with the score still at 2–2, it was difficult to visualise Leeds not eventually getting their hands on the trophy.

For the replay at Old Trafford, Chelsea, anxious to find a way to stop Gray, switched Harris to right-back and moved Webb to the heart of their defence alongside Dempsey. However, while Gray was not as consistently dangerous as he had been at Wembley, this was more than offset by the problems that Peter Lorimer created for Chelsea down the other flank, and Clarke and Jones through the middle. It was Jones who put them ahead just before half-time, following a Gray-type run by Clarke past three Chelsea defenders. By that stage, Chelsea had not had one shot and the more the game progressed, the more their chances of getting back into the match seemed to evaporate. But 15 minutes from the end, Osgood, from a delicate Charlie Cooke chip into the space behind the Leeds back-four, struck with a flying header. The goal was like a huge dose of adrenalin to Chelsea, while Leeds wilted, clearly horror-stricken. So, with this titanic clash again going into extra-time, Chelsea could confidently set their sights on more than merely survival.

If there is one goal that will always haunt Leeds fans, it was the one that finally crushed Leeds five minutes before the end of extra-time. The memory is particularly emotive for Gray, if only because of who scored it. Hutchinson, who could hurl the ball almost as far as some players could kick it, propelled a long throw into the near post area of the Leeds goal; Charlton, misjudging the flight of the ball, mis-headed it high to the far post, and there was Webb making up for all that torment he had suffered at Wembley to put it in the net.

It is typical of Gray that, despite the disappointment and sense of injustice he experienced over that result, he readily acknowledges the praise Webb deserved 'in getting the last laugh'. As Gray says: 'You've got to give him credit. OK, I got the better of him at Wembley, but the thing about him in that match that I respected was the way he stuck to his job. I thought he showed tremendous character.' The courage to play, indeed.

That courage helped Gray turn in numerous performances of which any footballer in the world would have been proud. However, the one that the football followers he meets most want to talk about is the 1970 FA Cup final, was one of the few post-war finals that lived up to expectations. Dr Andrew Stephen, the Football Association chairman at the time, said: 'This was a classic, an epic. Believe me, we need this kind of show to make the final a showpiece.' He went on to describe Leeds's display as being 'in the World Cup class'.

Even Leeds's biggest detractors could not dispute that this certainly applied to Eddie Gray.

6

Allan Clarke

At around 4.10 p.m. on Saturday, 6 May 1972, Allan Clarke scored one of the most memorable goals in Leeds United's 77-year history.

The high quality of the goal, like a stunning picture requiring an appropriate frame, had the perfect setting: the Centenary FA Cup final at Wembley, against United's old London adversaries, Arsenal. For Leeds, it couldn't have been more precious; Clarke's dramatic diving header, from a cross by his striking partner, Mick Jones, was the only goal of the game and brought the trophy to Leeds for the first time. The fact that it was achieved at Arsenal's expense was sweet revenge for the blow that the Gunners had inflicted upon Leeds the previous season, when they pipped them for the Championship, and left them with the unenviable distinction of being the first team under the two points for a win system to finish First Division runners-up with a total as high as 64. Leeds, having been sensationally bundled out of the FA Cup by Colchester in the fifth round, had also had to endure the sight of Arsenal winning the FA Cup to become only the second team this century to land the double.

Of course, Leeds's euphoria did not last long – 48 hours later, their dreams of emulating Arsenal's double triumph evaporated in a defeat at Wolves, a match from which they needed only a point to clinch the title at the expense of Derby and Liverpool. However, the memory of their superb show against Arsenal at Wembley proved much more enduring. One of the great things about it for Leeds was the effect it had on their image. The performance enabled the club to take another step towards becoming firmly established in the minds of the general public as a team who deserved to be loved as well as respected, a team who could win trophies in style.

It had taken Leeds some time to get to that position. In the early stages of their development, the great team that Don Revie built was noted not so much for their skill, but for an approach to the game that seemed to take professionalism to the extreme. In terms of gamesmanship, Leeds knew every trick in the book. They could be ruthlessly combative and, for a team with so many skilful players, infuriatingly inhibited. However, the first step towards bringing a more relaxed element into their play came in 1969 when they won the Championship for the first time. It was from that point that their players truly began to be given greater freedom to express their talents and develop the creative aspects of their game, as reflected by their signing of a master finisher of Clarke's calibre from Leicester in June 1969 for a then British record transfer fee of £165,000.

Clarke, who spent nine years at Leeds as a player and two as the manager – from 1980 to 1982 – says: 'It puzzles me a bit when I hear Billy Bremner [one of his closest friends] talk about the Leeds players being taken off the leash because I can't remember their being restricted in any way. Before matches against Leeds with my previous clubs, I'd heard managers say: "If you try and play their type of football, they'll absolutely murder you, so you're going to have to rough them up a bit." However you wanted to play against Leeds was fine by them. If you wanted to play them at football, they would play football and stuff you. If you wanted to turn it into a physical battle, they would stuff you at that, too. The change that Billy and others refer to must have taken place when I joined because I tell you now, the football that team played in the time I was there was the best football you will ever see in your life.'

Nonetheless, Clarke had to wait to fully reap the benefits of this. A member of the Leicester team beaten by Manchester City in the 1969 Cup final (a blow compounded by their relegation to the Second Division), he must have felt he was fated to be denied a winners' medal in this competition. The following year, Leeds were held 2–2 by Chelsea at Wembley, after twice being ahead, and lost the lead again in the replay at Old Trafford before crashing 2–1. He might also have been struck by the thought that he was destined to experience the same anguish in all the other competitions, too. That season, as if the defeat by Chelsea wasn't hard enough to take, Leeds were runners-up in the Championship, and lost to Celtic in the European Cup semi-finals. Though the 1970/71 season followed the same pattern, it did end on the high note of a 3–3 aggregate draw against Juventus in the Inter Cities Fairs Cup final, and ultimate victory for Leeds on the away goal rule. Clarke was one of the scorers in the final. It was rare that he was not on the scoreboard in any of his Leeds games. However, it was the goal he scored against Arsenal at Wembley for which he will always be best remembered.

In view of the tight, ultra-competitive nature of previous Leeds–Arsenal battles, including the war of attrition that represented Leeds's 1–0 win over the Gunners in the 1968 League Cup final, it did not need a soothsayer to predict that it would take something special to separate the two teams. Equally predictable, perhaps, was that Clarke, nicknamed 'Sniffer' because of his ability to find openings, in situations where none appeared to exist, was one of the Leeds stars most liable to provide it.

At first glance, Clarke, born (on 31 July 1946) and raised near Willenhall, Staffordshire, was not the most imposing of figures. At 6ft and 11 stone, he was built like a pipe cleaner; and the initial impression of him as a player who could be easily crushed was further highlighted by his pale, boyish features. But Clarke was physically stronger than he looked, as opponents who attempted to intimidate him physically quickly discovered. As Clarke says, if referees did not give him 'protection' against those who sought to clog him out of a game, he was quite capable of taking the law into his own hands. 'My attitude was: "Well, you might kick me twice, but the third time, watch out." It was something I learned over the years – the importance of the centre-half showing you respect. I found that once you started giving the centre-half some stick, he would back off and you would get more room to play.' The team-mates who teased him about his build also found Clarke invariably having the last word. 'They used to pull my leg blind about my weight,' Clarke recalls. 'I only put on about five pounds in the close season, and in pre-season training, that came off on the first day. It was great once we started doing cross-country runs because I would be motoring along, no problem, whereas they would be spewing their hearts out.'

Other characteristics that caused him to stand out as a top-class striker were his single-mindedness and self-confidence, plus his first touch, and his composure under pressure. That composure, reflecting a cold, calculating football brain, would have boosted the firing line of any team. Clarke, indeed, had emphasised the point in the middle-of-the-range or struggling teams in which he had played at his three previous clubs. After coming to the fore at Walsall, where he started as a 15-year-old apprentice in 1961 and scored 41 goals in 72 League matches, he scored 45 goals in only 85 matches for Fulham, and 12 in 36 for Leicester. Given Clarke's determination to establish himself in the England team, and Leicester's unenviable double the season before, Clarke left them for Leeds; the opportunity at last to reverse his position of being a big fish in a small pond came at a good time for him. It came at a good time for Leeds, too. With Clarke's delicate skills complementing the physical power of Jones perfectly, Leeds gained the sharpest of cutting edges to their mesmerising approach play. In addition to his being Leeds's top scorer in four of his nine seasons at Elland Road, it says much about the clinical aspect of Clarke's finishing skills that his scoring average for Leeds was a goal every two games over 151 matches.

What made him so good? Part of the answer lies in his personality and temperament. At Fulham and Leicester, he tended to stand out as a man apart, an image which did not always endear him to his team-mates. The leading light of a big footballing family – his brothers, Wayne, Frank, Derek and Kelvin also played League football – he was looked upon as being difficult to get on with, self-centred and arrogant. He, though, suggests this was partly because he cared more about winning than other players. 'I was a winner, and the players I worked with at Leeds were winners, too,' he explains. 'At Fulham and Leicester you'd sometimes see players laughing in the bath after a defeat. Now I couldn't do that – I couldn't accept it. The press described me as a loner for that reason, but I'm sorry – if that made me a loner, so be it. While I liked a laugh and a joke as much as anybody, I took my football seriously. I had a job of work to do and I gave it everything I had. That was the way I was; that was my character. It was one of the reasons why I think I felt so much at home at Leeds. They lost far fewer games than my other clubs did, but when Leeds got beat, the dressing-room would be like a morgue. To me, that's how it should have been. You know what I mean? You don't laugh when you get beat. My attitude had always made me good for a story at Leicester, and after about six months at Leeds, I remember the press coming up to me in the hope that I might say something controversial again. But I said: "I've got nothing to say. I am among winners – I'm happy".'

The more meaningful manner in which this was expressed was through his performances. Clarke, never a shrinking violet over assessments of his ability, is more lucid than ever today on the subject of the self-assurance he showed with Leeds:

There is a lot of pressure on goalscorers, but I never allowed this to affect me. I never suffered from nerves as such – the adrenalin would be pumping, but I was never uptight. The bigger the game, the bigger the stage, the more I loved it. If I missed chances, I would only think about them after a game, when I got to bed that night. Even after matches in which I had scored two or three, I would be inclined to think more about the chances that I didn't stick away. But, during a game, my attitude was: 'So what? You should have scored there, but you'll tuck away the next chance.'

The one thing that the gaffer always said to me was: 'If you've only got one man to beat to get in a shot, Allan, just shake your body, go past him and stick the ball in the net.' It never seemed to occur to him that it might not come off for me. He used to say that if ever I got into that position in a match, or if I had only the goalkeeper in front of me, he could sit back and relax, knowing that it was bound to be a goal. Actually, I fancied my chances in that situation anyway, but I used to think: 'Christ, he must think I am great.' Whether you can call it motivation, I don't know, but it certainly gave me a lift.

The thing about it was that I didn't let difficult shooting angles worry me. People in the game look upon it as a crime for goalkeepers to get beaten on their near post, but I got loads of near-post goals. More often than not, I would hit the ball with the inside of my foot, to get the maximum degree of accuracy, and I think a lot of keepers might have been surprised at the power I was able to get into my shots that way. It was a natural thing. It wasn't something that I worked on. It came in particularly handy in one against one situations with the keeper. They are not as easy for the striker as they might look, because you are conscious of opposing defenders trying to catch up with you to get in a tackle, and you've got the keeper coming off his line to narrow your shooting angle.

It was a battle of wits, a battle of nerve. As the keeper was moving towards me, I knew that there had to be a point at which he would have to stop, and I was quite happy to wait for that moment. He might have been virtually right on top of me, maybe no more than ten yards away, but as soon as he stopped that was the moment I shot. Not only this, I used to concentrate on hitting the ball low and as close to the keeper as possible, knowing that he was going to struggle to get down to it quickly enough. David Harvey [the Leeds goalkeeper] will tell you about this. I was only the third-choice penalty taker at Leeds, but I still used to practise taking them against Dave in training. One of the first things I looked for in matches was whether the opposing keeper was naturally right- or left-handed – you could tell just by noting the hand with which he threw the ball in the pre-match kick-in. Nine times out of ten, I would hit the ball to his right if he was left-handed and to his left if he was right-handed. Dave is right-handed, and before I took penalties against him in training, I actually told him where I was going to place the ball, and he still couldn't stop them. Then he would position himself a yard further towards that post, then another yard, and eventually, he was so close to the post that he could almost touch it. Even then, while he would save the odd one, I scored more than I missed.

Clarke's ball skills and balance, his ability to involve himself in the overall build-up play, made him more than merely a finisher. 'When Leeds bought me,' he argues, 'they did not buy a goalscorer, they bought a footballer. To my mind, great strikers should not only be able to score a lot of goals, they should be able to make a lot of goals for others as well. This is why I believe that Alan Shearer is way out in front of all the other present-day British strikers. Yes, he's a goalscorer. But he's also a footballer.' In both contexts, Clarke, now working for a ventilation company, had cause to be grateful for the company of the likes of John Giles, Billy Bremner and Eddie Gray:

Being with so many outstanding players improved my game, if only because of the way they dominated teams and the number of chances they created. They also helped me develop as an all-round striker. I can honestly say that with Leeds, I worked ten times harder than I did at my previous clubs. It wasn't that I didn't want to do it with Fulham and Leicester; it was just that no one there said anything to me about my approach to the game. At Leeds, it was expected of you, the players there actually demanded that you pull your weight on behalf of the team, on and off the ball, and both in attack and defence. I remember Billy Bremner telling me that he never realised that Mick Jones and I worked so hard in the FA Cup final against Arsenal until he watched it on the video. He says: 'You and Mick must have covered every blade of grass on the Wembley pitch.'

The experience of playing for United in Europe had a lot to do with it, I think. When you are playing a European tie away from home, you are up against everything – I'm not just talking about the opposing team, but also the referees and linesmen, the home supporters. Even our team had its back to the wall in some matches and, on the basis of your attack being the first line of defence, Mick and I had to spend a lot of our time just closing opponents down and helping the team keep things tight. In Europe, we had to contend with being man-for-man marked, which was something that took me time to get used to. I used to get so frustrated. As soon as we kicked off, I knew that the man detailed to mark me would be with me for the full 90 minutes. Italian defenders were particularly disciplined in this role. At the end of one match, I actually said to my marker: 'Are you coming in the bath with me as well?' After a while, though, I learned to turn this to the team's advantage. I learnt to draw markers out of position, to make room for Gilesey or Billy to go into. It was all part of the learning process.

The biggest compliment I could pay to Giles was that when it came to passing the ball, he was the nearest to Johnny Haynes that I have ever seen. I was 19 when I played with Haynes at Fulham, and every time I made a good run for the ball, you could bet that he would get it to me. Giles was the same, as was Billy. The ball was there for me, exactly how I wanted it, and all I had to do was stick it in the net. Look, I don't want to make it seem as if goalscoring is easy – it isn't – but it was a piece of cake at Leeds because you were playing with so many great players. Great players make the game look simple because they play it simple – that's the art of it. No matter what the position in which you received possession, you always had not one player available for a pass, but two or three. So that was another reason why I feel I became a more complete player at Leeds. The best way I can sum it up is to say that when I played for England, the only instructions I got from Sir Alf Ramsey were: 'Play like you do for Leeds United.' That's all he ever really said to me.

Of course, of all the stars who played a part in Clarke's success at Elland Road, Jones, who arrived at Leeds (via Sheffield United) almost two years earlier, deserves to be at the very top of the list. The Worksop-born Jones was a centre-forward in the traditional British target man mould. His courage, selfless running and power in the air often enabled him to get to balls that other strikers would have given up on, and as Don Revie once said of him: 'He does not give centre-halves a moment's peace. There isn't a centre-half in Britain who is not happy to hear the final whistle after playing against Mick.'

Jones, the less glamorous member of the duo – he gained only three England caps, compared to Clarke's 19 – was not the sort of person to allow personal ego to get in the way of his performances. Jones was essentially quiet and self-effacing, a player who thought nothing of sacrificing himself in the interests of his team. One way in which his devotion to the Leeds cause could be measured was that he was reckoned to be one of the Elland Road stars who had the fewest reservations about playing, and playing flat out, when not fully match fit. This was a common problem among all the Leeds players at that time. Leeds played more competitive matches than any other First Division club, and towards the end of the season, a make-or-break period when they needed a full-strength team more than ever, it was not unusual for men like Jones to go into action with injuries necessitating pain-killing injections.

Jones's easy-going nature was affected in other ways. Clarke says that he and Bremner repeatedly 'wound him up' about his clothes, especially after Jones happened to come in for training one day inadvertently wearing trousers too short for him. 'I think it got to the stage where, before Mick left his house, he'd ask his wife Glynis if he looked all right,' Clarke says, laughing. 'He used to get changed next to Bill and myself, and would not arrive until the last moment – he used to walk through the dressing-room door at about two minutes to ten, by which time we were all in our training gear. But Bill and I were ready for him – I think he was a nervous wreck by the time we'd finished with him. He was a smashing bloke. You couldn't fall out with him even if you tried. You know, if something happened in training, he would just laugh at you. I've never known anyone like him.' That comment is certainly valid in the sense of how Jones, who generally took up the most advanced position when Leeds were on the attack and was often the first player they would try to 'hit' from defence or midfield, helped Clarke on the field. Clarke says: 'Yeah, Mick was the leader of the line if you like – he was absolutely magnificent at that – whereas I used to drop short and feed off him. When I joined Leeds, I thought it would take about 12 months for us to get used to each other, but I'm not joking, we clicked straight away. He could immediately read me and vice versa. Unbelievable. For example, if Leeds were developing an attack down the right or left, one of us would be heading for the far post and the other for the near post. Mick was usually the one to go to the far post, but we didn't actually work on this in training. We more or less sorted things out ourselves. You never really saw Mick and myself going for the same ball. We balanced off each other right from the word go.'

It was a balancing act that stood Leeds in particularly good stead in the 1971/72 season, following an erratic start comprising five wins, three draws and four defeats, and a gamble by Revie in bringing the injured Clarke and Jones back into the team rather sooner than his training staff deemed advisable. Leeds had been forced to play their opening eight League matches away from home, the Football Association punishment (combined with a hefty fine) meted out to them because of the crowd misconduct during their controversial 2–1 defeat by West Bromwich Albion at Elland Road the previous season. Revie felt that the defeat, or rather the hotly disputed refereeing decision that prompted it, was the major factor in causing Leeds to be beaten by Arsenal in the Championship race.

Renowned as a worrier, as a man whose emotions were invariably laid bare for all to see, Revie was in a similarly angry mood on 9 October 1971, when Leeds lost 3–1 at Coventry. It was not so much the scoreline that upset Revie but the manner in which it was achieved. He was so upset by the performances of his players that he even thought about resigning.

Revie, talking shortly after Leeds's triumph over Arsenal at Wembley, said: 'At the time of our defeat by Coventry, I honestly believed that this Leeds team would not win anything, and that for the first time in many years, we wouldn't even get close to doing so. That defeat made me feel ashamed of the team. At the final whistle, I turned to Les Cocker [Leeds's trainer] and said: "I've never seen a sloppier performance from our lads. They look as if they have gone." One of the secrets of Leeds's success over the years is that, when things haven't been going right for us technically, we have at least rolled up our sleeves and battled. So it was disturbing to me that we appeared to have lost even that.

'I actually felt that maybe we had all been together for too long, and that I should make way for a new manager with different ideas. In our team talk after the match, I told the players: "If you reckon we have gone as far as we can together, I am quite willing to move on."' The following Wednesday, Revie, having returned from a three-day holiday in Jersey with his wife, Elsie, delivered an 'improve or I quit' ultimatum to his players, and decided that Clarke and Jones, out of action with groin and hamstring injuries, had to be brought back as quickly as possible.

'How long will it take to get them fully fit?' Revie asked the club's physiotherapist, Bob English, that morning. 'About a fortnight,' he replied. 'After they've finished their treatment today, they'll be having hot and cold baths, and remedial exercises.' 'Not this morning,' Revie told him. 'They are going to train with the rest of the lads because I want them to play on Saturday [at home to Manchester City].'

Revie recalled that Jones, Clarke and English looked at him 'as if I was mad'. The only previous occasion he had taken this sort of risk, he added, was for Leeds's second FA Cup fifth-round replay against Sunderland in 1967 when Bremner, suffering from a knee ligament injury, 'played virtually on one leg' but created the chance from which Jack Charlton scored the winning goal. The gamble with Clarke and Jones also paid off, with the two men finding the net and Leeds producing their most sparkling form for months to romp home 3–0. 'That for me was Leeds's turning point that season,' Revie said, pointing out that Leeds, in addition to reaching the FA Cup final, won 18 and lost only five of their remaining 29 matches, and came agonisingly close to winning the Championship. It was during that season that Leeds produced performances of which any team in the world would have been proud with their 5–1 win over Manchester United, and that famous 7–0 thrashing of Southampton.

All of which emphasised the advantages of a team not having too much on their plates, even one with the strength in depth of Leeds. They had been knocked out of the UEFA and League Cup competitions in the early rounds, which gave their players more breathing space to build themselves up physically and mentally for the two other major competitions in which they were involved.

The road to Wembley began with a comfortable 4–1 win over Bristol Rovers. Clarke wasn't on the scoresheet that day, but as if to emphasise his ability to destroy the best teams, he scored both goals in Leeds's 2–0 home win against Liverpool in the fourth round, following a goalless draw at Anfield, and got the first goal in the 2–1 sixth-round win at Tottenham.

In addition to Clarke's part in the Liverpool triumph, the matches were something of a turning point for Leeds's veteran centre-half, Jack Charlton. Prior to the first Leeds–Liverpool clash, Charlton had not played well in a League match at Tottenham, and for days Revie wrestled with the dilemma of whether to drop him. It wasn't until the morning of the Anfield clash that he finally elected to do so, switching Paul Madeley from right-back to centre-half and telling the media that Charlton had flu to save his redoubtable old warrior any public embarrassment. But Charlton was back in the team by the time they were due to face Liverpool again, and as Revie said: 'He never put a foot wrong. I felt Jack had reached a stage in his career where he needed to be dropped from time to time. When you have spent 20 years as a pro, as he had done, it is not easy to keep raising your game week in week out. Being left out against Liverpool was a blow to his pride. He never put a foot wrong from then on. Indeed, I don't think Jack ever played better than he did at Wembley. Two days short of his 37th birthday, I think he realised this was maybe his last chance to get an FA Cup winners' medal, and he was prepared to die in the attempt if necessary.' The extent to which Charlton was keyed up for the game became apparent to Revie in a training session the day before the final. 'How do you feel about tomorrow, boss?' Charlton asked him. 'This might surprise you, Jack, but I have never felt more confident in my life,' Revie replied. 'I don't,' Charlton said. 'I feel dead nervous.' Later, Revie confided to Les Cocker: 'I think Jack's going to have a blinder tomorrow. When he's nervous, he's right on top of his game.'

But, as ever, there were no signs of nerves from Clarke, who was determined that he was going to enjoy the occasion, and to remember every kick. 'I can remember the match as if it took place yesterday,' he says. 'A lot of players say that when taking part in a cup final for the first time, the whole occasion seems to go by very quickly and you don't really take it in. That was definitely the case with me when I played for Leicester in the 1969 final – afterwards, I could hardly remember anything about it. But the more times you play in the final, the more you can savour the experience. I thoroughly enjoyed the 1970 FA Cup final, even though we eventually got beat, and I enjoyed the 1972 one even more.'

At their London hotel on the eve of the match, the Leeds team could hardly have failed to get into the right frame of mind while they watched a video of their 7–0 thrashing of Southampton. Clarke and Bremner, who complemented each other as effectively as Little and Large when joining forces to indulge in dressing-room fun and games, also lightened the atmosphere in the Leeds camp, at the expense of a man called Herbert Warner.

By trade, Warner, now in his eighties, sold jewellery from a stall in Barnsley Market. As an avid Leeds United fan, and a close friend of Revie, he also became a much-loved – and important – member of the United family. Warner, a man with a warm, gregarious personality, was a sort of general factotum to the players in the dressing-room before matches, helping them to focus their attention on their jobs without any distractions. In some ways, he could be described as something of a dressing-room court jester, and with men like Clarke and Bremner around, it was a role which required a thick skin. Clarke recalls one period when the boredom of journeys for away matches was relieved by Bremner and himself goading Warner into trying to outsprint the coach driver over 100 yards. As Warner was much older than his rival, there was only going to be one winner – even after Bremner and Clarke, having watched Warner give a passable impression of Jim Peters just before the athlete collapsed in the Olympic marathon, agreed to give him a ten-yard start. But the pair, emphasising the cutting sense of humour common in the laddish world of professional football, clearly enjoyed the sight of his discomfort. 'He could easily have had a heart attack,' Clarke laughs. 'Oh, he is a lovely man. You could have a lot of fun with him, without him ever really taking offence. If he did get upset, it didn't last long – you could be sure that he would be there again the following week. The wind-ups with Herbert had me and Billy killing ourselves laughing before matches. He was great for our morale.'

The point was illustrated particularly vividly on the eve of the clash with Arsenal, when Gabby Harris, another friend of Revie's, presented the players with silver trays to mark their achievement, and Warner followed suit with the gift of personalised tankards. 'He'd even gone to the trouble of writing a poem to go with each one,' Clarke says. 'He was quite emotional, but you should have seen his face when we said to him: "Is that all you're giving us, Herbert?" You know, we compared the present he had given us with the one we'd got from Gabby, and for a moment or two, he actually took us seriously – we put on a great act and had him going. It was very funny at the time, and it was typical of him that he saw the funny side of it, too.'

Revie also had cause to smile. He felt that Arsenal would miss the know-how of their experienced Scottish international goalkeeper, Bob Wilson, who had suffered cartilage trouble shortly before the final and been replaced by Geoff Barnett. On the face of it, the same point could have been made about Leeds's goalkeeper David Harvey, who had displaced Gary Sprake and, like Barnett, was making his first Wembley appearance. However, to Revie, Barnett had yet to show signs of instilling as much confidence in his team-mates as Wilson had done, and indeed Harvey had done. In his final dossier on Arsenal's strengths and weaknesses, handed to the players to study the day before the game, he wrote: 'All corners must be put under the bar. Don't foul the keeper as all that will do is help him out of situations where he has not looked that good. Just jump strong and as high as you can. Talk to the referee if he tries to protect Barnett too much, and do it in a nice quiet way by saying that it's not your fault if they don't have a top-class keeper.'

There was also much encouragement for Revie with the news of Arsenal electing not to put striker Ray Kennedy in their starting line-up. Recalling the success of the

Kennedy–John Radford partnership up front when the Gunners landed the 1971 Championship–FA Cup double, Revie said: 'Many people were contemptuous of Arsenal's direct style of play then, their tendency to keep hitting long balls up to Kennedy and Radford, thus by-passing midfield. But even if the big fellows failed to score from those balls, they could always be relied upon to prevent defenders getting the ball away cleanly. They put you under so much pressure. The signing of Alan Ball from Everton [in the 1971/72 season] and the dropping of Kennedy enabled Arsenal to develop a more constructive style of attacking play. They became a more attractive footballing team, but I am not sure that they did not lose some of their effectiveness as a result. At Wembley, we knew Ball would come deep to take short passes from his defence, and that he was not the type to produce long, telling balls from those positions, like John Giles could. So I always felt comfortable that, if Leeds lost the ball, we would have enough time to get ourselves organised properly defensively.' Revie's dossier had this to say on the subject:

> The back men of Arsenal were always looking to give him [Ball] the ball [in an Arsenal match against Stoke]. This led to a rather slow build-up in an extremely short game for Arsenal. In the past, the long ball to the big, strong front runners was their strong point. But now Arsenal do not really work with a definite front runner as both John Radford and Charlie George keep coming back deep, Radford especially. The high balls to George were a waste of time. I don't think they can match us skill-wise. In the match against Stoke, Arsenal were made to look a very ordinary side by Stoke not dwelling on the ball, keeping it free.
>
> Keep calm and think clearly. Don't let them upset you by niggling, kicking or trying to talk you out of it. Play your own confident, quick, brilliant football that you have been playing all season. This will sicken them more than getting involved with individual players.
>
> Billy Bremner got involved in the England–Scotland match [with Arsenal's combative midfielder, Peter Storey] and forgot

his responsibilities towards Scotland's team that day. You do this at times, Allan. Don't be drawn into situations of this kind. Let your ability talk.

Revie also felt that Arsenal's left-back, Bob McNab, was 'inclined to sell himself in the tackle'. As for the central defenders, Frank McLintock and Peter Simpson, he wrote that the pair 'don't take up good positions' to deal with opposing players connecting with balls cut back from the goal-line. To varying degrees, these observations were borne out by the Leeds goal, a deserved reward for the edge they had in technical ability and assertiveness.

The longer the game progressed, the more dominant Leeds became. This certainly applied to Clarke. Subjected to a late fitness test because of a groin injury, he admits that he did not feel entirely comfortable at the start. 'It was a very hot day,' he explains, 'and in the first five minutes or so, your mouth is dry and you're thinking: "Christ, I need some oxygen here." But then through the concentration you are putting in, you soon forget about it and get a second wind.' In Clarke's case, this was borne out by his willingness to start running at Arsenal defenders with the ball from deep positions. 'I don't know why I did it – in normal circumstances, I was the type who would lay the ball off rather than go forward with it, taking on people. But the first time I did it, it was obvious that they didn't like it.'

Arsenal, who had been the first to threaten a goal, with a Ball shot which Paul Reaney cleared off the line, were certainly panicking when Clarke, from a pass by Bremner, carried the ball forward from inside the Leeds area to the edge of the Gunners' box. Clarke, prevented from creating the space he needed for a shot, managed to slip the ball to Jones, who fired no more than a yard wide. Clarke came even closer to scoring when, reacting superbly to an intended Lorimer shot from the right which turned into a powerful cross beyond the far post, he propelled a header against the bar. 'When things like that happen, you think that it is not going to be your day,' he says.

One of his memories of the goal that eradicated this fear concerns the pain he was experiencing following a tangle with McLintock, in which the Arsenal captain accidentally trod on his fingers. 'It didn't half hurt like.' But that was inevitably pushed to the back of his mind as passes by Paul Madeley and Peter Lorimer transferred the ball from the left to the right – to Jones – and Clarke scrambled to his feet to add his presence to the players pushing up in support of the striker. Jones's power and determination enabled him to edge past McNab and, just when it seemed that he might have run the ball out of play, he produced a cross which eluded the Arsenal defence and started dropping by the penalty spot. Clarke, having made a diagonal run towards it from the left of the penalty area, recalls: 'As the ball's in flight, I am thinking: "Try for a volley." I've made up my mind to hit it on the volley with my right foot. But suddenly, I realised that the ball was going to drop earlier than I had expected, and I knew that if I let that ball drop on the floor, Pat Rice [the Arsenal right-back who was striving to cover his run] would be right on top of me and the chance would be gone.' Hence the fact that Clarke threw himself at the ball to produce a perfect low header into the right of the net.

Arsenal could well have equalised – George hit the bar – but there was no doubting Leeds's right to get their hands on the famous trophy at last. Terry Brindle of the *Yorkshire Post* wrote: 'It was the day on which Leeds proved beyond question that they are a great team.' Even the London media, somewhat critical of Leeds in the past, shared that view. Frank Butler, the sports editor of the *News of the World*, wrote: 'Leeds had always looked the more classy footballing side. Once they scored, they blossomed out like supermen.'

As Leeds had another mountain to climb 48 hours later, at Wolves, the celebrations of the team, unlike those of their followers, were somewhat muted. While the club's FA Cup final banquet went ahead on the Saturday night, the players were absent. Still, if nothing else, the glow of their Wembley triumph served as a more than reasonable burst of sunshine to keep them warm amid the cold winds that were to follow. The dark clouds started forming even before the final whistle at Wembley, when Jones, while again getting around the back of the Arsenal defence on the right a couple of minutes from the end, collided with Barnett and dislocated his shoulder. The injury meant his missing the crucial Wolves match, a blow to the club which Revie himself readily endorsed when he said: 'Mick's ability to hold the ball under pressure long enough for colleagues to move up in support makes him one of our most vital players in away matches.'

Equally disconcerting to Leeds, who needed a point to clinch the Championship, there was also some doubt about the fitness of Clarke, who aggravated his groin injury at Wembley and was undergoing intensive treatment. Clarke did play, as did two others who had been nursing injuries, John Giles and Eddie Gray. All three had to have pain-killing injections.

At the finish, they needed them for their hearts, let alone their limbs. Leeds were denied what looked a clear penalty, when Bernard Shaw handled the ball to prevent Clarke pouncing on a rebound from the Wolves keeper Phil Parkes – and lost 2–1. Clarke had been forced to go off half an hour from the end, shortly after Bremner had reduced the arrears to give Leeds a ray of hope, and as Revie said: 'When Allan went, our chances of getting an equaliser went with him.'

So, with Liverpool also faltering that night – ironically, they failed to get the win they needed at Arsenal – Derby, whose team was abroad on a club holiday at the time, were champions, and Leeds runners-up for the fifth time in eight seasons. Of course, Leeds should not have been forced to play a match of this importance so soon after the FA Cup final. Initially, it was intended to play it on Thursday, 18 May; but with England due to face Wales at Wembley on 20 May, their manager, Sir Alf Ramsey, refused to allow the Leeds players in his squad, Madeley and Norman Hunter, to be released.

'Few people fully appreciate how much playing in an FA Cup final can take out of players,' Revie pointed out. 'The tension of the occasion alone can sap their stamina. The problem was really driven home to me on the eve of the Wolves match, when a number of the players complained that their legs felt heavy. It was the first time I had ever known them to intimate that they were tired before such an important game.' Some argued that Revie could have done more to help his team – and Clarke especially – by replacing Jones with Joe Jordan, then his reserve centre-forward, and a similar player to Jones. But, on the grounds of Jordan's lack of big-match experience, Revie brought Mick Bates into the side in midfield and switched Bremner to the front. Referring to the Shaw handball controversy, Revie commented: 'I thought he was going to stuff it up his jersey.' However, to Revie and the Leeds players, it was a refereeing mistake which was mainly responsible for their sad end to the season.

That night at Molineux did not signal the end of such hard-luck stories for Clarke and Leeds. There was, of course, the 1975 European Cup final against Bayern Munich, in which Clarke was again one of the central figures in a controversial decision not to award Leeds a first-half penalty when he was brought down in an easy scoring position by Franz Beckenbauer, and Bayern went on to win 2–0. 'I was definitely going to score, no question about that. I took Beckenbauer on, got past him, and with only Sepp Maier to beat, I knew exactly where I was going to place the ball. But as I was about to shoot, Beckenbauer just wrapped his legs around me.'

All this, however, was more than offset by the goals Clarke scored – notably the one against Arsenal at Wembley – and his contentment at being in a team able to help him get the maximum out of his outstanding ability: 'When people ask me what my most cherished Leeds memory is, they automatically assume it must be the 1972 FA Cup final,' he says. 'But I'll tell you what it is . . . it is the buzz I got in those days just by going in for training. No matter what the weather, I couldn't wait to get to the ground each morning, and get into the five-a-sides. I mean, the one day a week that I hated was Sunday;

I just couldn't wait for Monday. The defenders loved those small-sided games, too, because they said they were the only matches in which they could get a decent number of touches on the ball. They said that in the competitive matches, all they did was win the ball, give it to the attacking players and sit back and admire what we did with it.

'Football-wise, I had the time of my life. I was with great players. I was with winners.'

7

Billy Bremner

On 7 November 1974, the crowd of 36,051 for Hibernian's UEFA Cup second-round second-leg tie against Leeds at Easter Road witnessed one of the strangest sights in British football, that of Billy Bremner, the little red-headed Leeds captain and midfield dynamo, lining up for the Yorkshire giants as a sweeper. They were also treated to one of the most audacious individual performances they could ever hope to see; a one-man show which summed up the all-round technical ability – not to mention the swaggering self-confidence – that brought this most inspiring of players more international caps than any other player in the club's history – 56 for Scotland – and more trophies than any other Leeds captain.

That Leeds were happy to play Bremner in defence, thus sacrificing his unrivalled ability to drive forward in support of the strikers and create vital goals, said much about the unimportance of this match to them. Bursting to wipe out the memory of their shock FA Cup final defeat by Sunderland the previous season, and conscious of their tendency in the past to fall into the trap of taking on too much, they had made up their minds to concentrate on the Championship. Hence the fact that the teams Don Revie selected for Leeds' early UEFA Cup and League Cup ties were rather different from the ones he put out in the First Division, and, that Leeds started the season with seven successive championship wins, then stretched their unbeaten League run to 29 matches and were nine points ahead of the field by the midway mark. When they faced Hibernian, following a 0–0 draw in the first leg at Elland Road, their attitude was that it would be good to get through, but that nobody would be shedding many tears if they didn't.

In some ways, the selection of Bremner in that unaccustomed role as the deepest member of the Leeds defence, despite the fact that he was unusually small for the spot, at 5ft 5ins, was the ultimate compliment to him. The top continental teams had thought nothing of putting their most talented creative players in that role, arguing that good football starts from the back and that being in such a deep position gave players the advantage of having more time and space on the ball than they could normally expect when operating further forward. The general view on this in Britain was more sceptical. Managers, coaches and players there had been conditioned to think of a sweeper being used in a defensive, negative way, as had been the case in Italy. Thus, when Franz Beckenbauer, having started his career as an outstanding attacking midfield player, switched to the sweeper role in the Bayern Munich and West Germany teams, it was perceived as an unforgivable waste of his ability. Many felt that being in this position gave such players the scope to perform too much within themselves, and that was Bremner's opinion, too. 'The gaffer told me that, if Leeds played with a sweeper regularly, he would have me there all the time, but I wasn't too impressed with that. You know, when people used to rave about Beckenbauer, I'd say: "Yeah, but anybody can play in that position." ' Today, this attitude comes through in the way that he talks about his own experience in the role. 'Everyone was raving about it after the game,' he says. 'Even years after the game, people would come up to me in Scotland, and say: "I was at the match against Hibernian, Billy, and you were absolutely unbelievable, the things you did with the ball." But to me, it was a doddle, too easy. I kept wanting to get forward and get involved in the play up the park, but because we had so many youngsters in the team I had to sit there. I found it boring, I really did.'

But his fellow Leeds players didn't. David Harvey, Norman Hunter, Paul Madeley, Gordon McQueen, John Giles and Mick Jones were all missing from the Leeds team that night, a situation which, despite Leeds's claims that the players concerned were injured or ill, did not go down too well among Hibernian fans. One newspaper north of the border suggested that Leeds had deliberately fielded a weakened team and that this was an 'insult' to Scotland. The team got even weaker. Leeds started with a 19-year-old keeper, John Shaw, making only his second first-team appearance, and then had to bring on the 17-year-old Glan Letheren for the second half as a result of Shaw suffering a fractured finger. 'The first ten minutes were nerve-racking,' he said afterwards, 'but once I got over that I became confident and the more the game went on, I really enjoyed it.' Letheren, in fact, became so absorbed in the game that by the time the match ended he had forgotten that he'd left the signet ring his girlfriend had given him inside the goal and it wasn't until he'd got changed in the dressing-room that he realised what he had done.

The panic he experienced was nothing compared to what Hibernian went through. Bored Bremner might have been, but what he did to relieve the boredom rendered it truly a performance to savour. No matter how Hibs tried to penetrate the Leeds defence, Bremner was always there to plug the gap, and frustrate them. At one point, it reached the stage where he even started tantalising their forwards, like a matador demoralising a bull. The feature of that aspect of his display came through a header from a corner, which Bremner stopped on the goal-line. In that situation, most other players would have elected to get the ball away quickly but Bremner just put his foot on it and invited the Hibs players to come and get it. 'It was hilarious. It was the last thing they expected me to do. "What the hell is happening?" they're thinking – you could see it on their faces. Every time someone made a move towards the ball, I shaped to lay it off and he stopped. Eventually, I just pushed the ball to one side and knocked it down the flank to somebody.'

Bremner's level of control was such that, for all the pressure Hibs exerted, the score stood at 0–0 at the end of 90 minutes, and after 30 minutes of extra-time. That took the teams into a penalty shoot-out, and gave Bremner another stage on which to outsmart Hibs. He recalls: 'Pat Stanton [the Hibernian captain and, like Bremner, a high-profile Scottish international] was taking the first penalty, and as he went past me to put the ball on the spot, I said: "Pat, if you miss, the crowd are going to bloody kill you." He said: "Eff off," but then he missed.' Bremner was also among the penalty-takers; he had the responsibility of taking the last kick, with the score at 4–4. Even then, he found the temptation to have some fun impossible to resist.

As Bremner put the ball down, he held up a finger to Stanton to signify that he was going to score, and as he started his run-up, he indulged in a battle of wits with Hibernian's goalkeeper, Gordon McArthur, by pointing to the right side of the goal. McArthur duly dived to that side, and was beaten by a shot to the other. But then one mitigating circumstance for him was that there was nothing in Bremner's run-up to suggest that he was not going to put the ball in the direction he had intimated. Indeed, to do otherwise, the right-footed Bremner, virtually square with the ball – to its left – when he struck it, would seemingly have needed to perform a minor miracle of agility to clip it across his body into the other corner. But this was an art in which Bremner specialised. 'I found it easy to cut balls back like that, especially with my passes,' he says. 'The gaffer used to say: "Christ, if anybody else tried to do that, he would end up with cartilage trouble." ' With Hibernian out of the UEFA Cup, Stanton, too, had something to say on the subject. 'You cocky little so and so,' he told Bremner.

Many other players who opposed Bremner during a

remarkable 17-year Leeds career in which he made 770 first-team appearances, just one short of the club record established by Jack Charlton, will have readily endorsed those sentiments. This side of Bremner, the side that took delight in expressing his skills to the extent of 'playing teams off the park', put him in very much the same category as those other outrageously gifted, gregarious Scottish football legends, Jimmy Johnstone and Jim Baxter, two of his all-time favourite players. Baxter himself gives a fascinating insight into the mentality of Bremner and himself when discussing their approach as Scotland team-mates in the famous 3–2 win over England at Wembley in 1967. Scotland were so much on top that Baxter teased the England players by juggling the ball in the air, and encouraging his colleagues to 'take the mickey out of them' with their own party tricks. According to Baxter, striker Denis Law took a dim view of this, arguing that if Scotland took the game seriously, they might even reverse the 9–3 scoreline they experienced on their previous Wembley visit. But Bremner was on Baxter's side. 'Aye, let's take the mickey out of them,' he agreed.

It was not only in that Hibernian match that Leeds's opponents were made to feel the same as England. There was that 7–0 win over Southampton in March 1972, when Bremner inevitably featured prominently in an awesome finale which saw Leeds stringing no fewer than 27 passes together without a Southampton player being able to get in a tackle. 'We weren't taking the mickey out of them,' Bremner protests. 'We were just trying to entertain our crowd.' Another 7–0 Leeds victory – at home to Chelsea in October 1967 – provided an even more impressive example of Bremner's sense of showmanship.

Chelsea were in turmoil following the resignation of their manager, Tommy Docherty, on the eve of the match and Bremner, making his last appearance for Leeds before starting a 28-day suspension for being sent off against Fulham the previous month, did more than anyone to make it worse. In his report in the *Yorkshire Evening Post*, Phil Brown wrote: 'At least Billy Bremner departed into the seclusion of suspension after playing one of the greatest games of his young life. Even if Chelsea could have offered more resistance than they did, he nevertheless reached the football heights. He showed just what a vintage champagne footballer he could be. His passes flowed like pieces of silk unrolling, releasing the taker into an opening perfectly, and his reverse pass [that pass clipped across his body] flashed several times to cut out a third of the defence.' Eric Stanger, of the *Yorkshire Post*, wrote: 'The man of the match was unquestionably Bremner. He teased and tormented them with his astonishing dexterity of foot and balance.' Moreover, having had a hand in Leeds's first two goals, and the fourth, Bremner got their last himself with a goal that was arguably the best of his career, a spectacular overhead 'bicycle' kick that brought the 40,460 house down. It also earned Leeds the record of being the first team to have seven different players on their scoresheet in a Football League match.

No team could intimidate Bremner, as was seen in the 1964/65 season, Leeds's first season back in the First Division. It seemed surprising to say the least that a side younger and less experienced than most of their rivals should come so close to achieving the double, finishing Championship runners-up to Manchester United on goal difference, and forcing Liverpool into extra-time in their FA Cup final defeat by the Merseyside club. Even in that company, however, Bremner, then just into his twenties, saw no reason why he should end up second best. Trust Bremner to get the goal that destroyed Manchester United's own hopes of achieving the double, in Leeds's 1–0 win over them in the semi-final replay; trust Bremner to have the temerity to cause jitters in the Liverpool camp by making it 1–1 against them near the end of normal time at Wembley.

You get vivid clues as to why such acts were typical of him when you listen to him on his experiences of playing for Scotland against the great Brazil teams and against Tottenham's Dave Mackay. He first played against Brazil in

Rio in 1972, when the Scots lost 1–0 after being so much on top that Bremner, on retrieving a ball that had gone out of play near the substitutes' bench, was moved to wind up the home players sitting there with obscene gestures. 'I was more or less saying to them: "I thought you lot could play like?" The Doc [manager Tommy Docherty] was loving it.' Not surprisingly, it was against Brazil in the 1974 World Cup finals in Germany that Bremner was on the receiving end of what he describes as the most painful foul of his career, a punch in the stomach by Rivelino, the Brazilian midfielder. 'I was dying,' Bremner recalls, adding proudly that when Rivelino then turned to check on the damage he had inflicted, he was able to hide the pain through a 'that didn't hurt a bit' grin. Bremner seems less gung-ho in that famous photograph of a snarling Mackay grabbing him by the neck, and almost lifting him off his feet, in a Tottenham–Leeds match. Bremner says he can't remember what provoked it. 'I wouldn't have picked on someone like Dave, sod that. All I can think of is that I did something to one of the other Tottenham players and he's reacted to it. Whenever I played against him, he seemed to take exception to me. A couple of times, I used to wonder: "Why is he so wound up about me – why is he not like that with anybody else?" The thing was, I admired him so much it wasn't true. I'd watched him playing for Hearts when I was a youngster, and I always wished that I could have played with him for Scotland.

'I don't think people realise how great a player Mackay was. Apart from his ability, he had a big heart. He was a warrior, you know what I mean?'

Warrior? Bremner was very much in that category himself, so one hardly needs to ask whether he was surprised that Leeds were able to establish themselves as a top First Division force so quickly. 'Us? Me? Christ, I never thought anybody was better than us, even when we had a crap team. I think a lot of the lads in our great team were like this. When we came up from the Second Division, everybody thought we would go straight back down again. The first game was at Aston Villa, and we won 2–1 after being a goal down. The next game, we beat Liverpool [the reigning champions] 4–0. It snowballed from there. We were only kids and we didn't give a monkey's about anything. After the games, particularly the tough games away from home, the fans would be shouting abuse at us, and we'd be telling them to eff off. When you look back on it, you think: "Christ, did we really do that? We're lucky we didn't get killed."

'I was never really a star-gazer, you know? I'd admire the top players I played against, the people like Pele, but I thought: "I don't care who he is – he's only got two legs and two arms." '

The point reminds Bremner of a conversation he had with his son, a professional golfer. Bremner junior, a teaching professional in Germany, felt that he had the ability to become a successful tournament player, but not the temperament and personality. Bremner says: 'When he was playing in big events, like the British Open and the Yorkshire Open, he said he did not want me to come and watch him because it might put too much pressure on him. Some time afterwards, he says to me: "As a player, you didn't care who was watching you or who you were playing with or against – you didn't give a monkey's about anybody. You know, Dad, if I'd had your personality, I might have gone a long way." '

This attitude made Bremner the ideal man around whom to build a successful team, as Don Revie noted. Indeed, if ever Revie could be said to have had any favourites among the players he nurtured as teenagers, then Bremner was surely at the top of the list. Revie was as protective towards them all as if they were his children, but Bremner, more headstrong and rebellious than the rest of the Leeds United family and less liable to be controlled by Revie in the manager's more possessive, dictatorial moments, tended to be viewed by him in a more liberal light. 'Aye, they called me his number two son [behind Revie's real one, Duncan],' Bremner says.

Peter Lorimer, Bremner's Leeds and Scotland team-mate, does not go so far as to say that Revie 'spoilt' Bremner.

Nonetheless, he says: 'If Billy had not played well, then to him, the whole team did not play well. That was the way he tended to think – he thought that Leeds United was all about Billy Bremner and ten others. That was the way Billy was, although I am not sure that Don didn't encourage him to think that way.' Lorimer recalls a match at West Ham, when the Leeds players were due to meet at the station for their Friday journey to London. 'All the lads are there – but not Billy. One of the lads says: "Look, I know he was having a night out in the town last night, and booked himself into the Griffin Hotel," and Don, having tried to reach him by phone, got someone to go across and get him. We were all sitting in the dining car when in walks Don, with Billy behind him. Now, Don, Billy, Jack Charlton and myself, the four of us, always played cards together on away trips, but Don has the needle with Billy, and he's sulking, really sulking. Billy said: "What's up with you lot? Won't I be all right for you tomorrow? If I don't do it tomorrow, you have a go at me then." Don still wouldn't play cards with him. After a while, he got up and sat somewhere else. But, sure enough, the next day at West Ham, Billy had a blinder, and the fact that he'd been late for the train and caused a panic was forgotten.'

This image of Bremner as a free spirit, or Leeds's irrepressible wild card, is endorsed by another Lorimer anecdote concerning his relationship with Jimmy Armfield, Leeds's manager from 1974 to 1978. Leeds, having lost to Bayern Munich in the 1975 European Cup final, had arranged a close season trip to Marbella, combining some matches there with a golfing holiday; and Bremner felt the need to unwind from the pressures of the season in his own way. The trip began with Bremner, having had a few 'bevvies', drawing everyone's attention to a newspaper report that Leeds were going to buy West Bromwich Albion's Len Cantello for £100,000, plus John Giles (Bremner's midfield partner) in exchange. 'Hey Jimmy,' Bremner shouted at Armfield, 'the wee man and a hundred grand for Cantello – has it not been printed wrong? Is it not a hundred grand and Cantello for the wee man?'

'Jimmy's just sitting there,' Lorimer recalls, marvelling over Bremner's cheekiness:

> Anyway, we get there [Marbella] and we go off into the town. We get back, and late that night, when Eddie [Gray] and I were in our rooms, we could hear shouting and bawling coming from the hotel grounds. We look over the balcony, and it's Billy and Clarkey. There had been some complaints from other residents, so the following morning, Jimmy got us all together – well 16 of the 18 players because Billy and Clarkey weren't there – and says: 'Our behaviour was diabolical last night. Any more of that and we're going home.' John [Giles] then asked who had been making the noise. 'Billy and Clarkey,' Jimmy says. 'Well, where are they?' John asked. 'They're not even here.' Jimmy told little Bob English [the Leeds physiotherapist] to go up to their room and bring them down, but ten minutes later Bob's back, looking very sheepish. 'Well, did you tell them to come down?' Jimmy asked. 'Yeah, I told them,' Bob replied. You could see that Bob was trying to evade the next part of it, what Bremner and Clarkey had said, but Jimmy dragged it out of him. 'Bob, what did they say?' Jimmy's said. 'Well, they said you've got to get lost, boss,' Jimmy's replied. The lads just burst out laughing. You know, when things like that happened, you just shook your head and thought: 'That Billy – what's he going to do or say next?' The guy was a one-off.

Armfield, like Bremner's other managers, deserves much credit for not attempting to destroy this side of the player. Lorimer himself readily concedes that all people are different, and that Bremner provided numerous examples to justify the willingness of everybody associated with him to accept him for the way he was. Certainly, the individualism that Bremner showed on the field proved far more a Leeds strength than a weakness. 'Billy was a great, great footballer,' Lorimer enthuses. 'Great ability, great temperament, great heart. To a point, you could say that there was a streak of indiscipline in the way that he played. I mean, if we got a goal behind, Billy straight-away thought he had to go up to centre-forward to get it back, as if nobody else was capable. Fortunately, we had someone in John Giles who could control things and enable us to adjust to it. If Billy went charging up, John would pull me inside, he'd pull Eddie inside – we'd compensate for it. Billy pulled so many matches out of the fire, it wasn't true. At the same time, there were odd times when you would think: "Don doesn't say anything to him when he charges into different positions, but he'd be going off his head if you were to do it." '

Not that Revie never went off his head with Bremner. There was a particularly explosive clash between the two during the early part of Bremner's Elland Road career, when Revie told him he was being switched from midfield to outside right. Bremner says: 'I told him: "I'll go on the park in that position, but I won't kick a ball for you there." He went berserk. He was banging that big fist of his on the table, and shouting that he would ban me, even finish me from football for life. I just said: "Please yourself – but I ain't playing wide on the right." ' Bremner admits that he did what he said he would do ('I never tried'). As for the fact that Revie's threats were not carried out, he says: 'You knew how far you could go with him.'

Bremner, like all the Leeds stars, was also aware that if he showed loyalty to Revie and Leeds, Revie would back him 100 per cent through thick and thin. Apart from his own experiences in that respect, Bremner gives an intriguing insight into this aspect of Revie's nature, and the 'chemistry' between the two men, when recalling his attitude to the players who tried their best for Leeds in their struggling days. One was a Glaswegian striker by the name of John McCole, who was bought for £10,000 from Bradford in September 1959 and played in the same Leeds team as Revie and Bremner. McCole, though managing to score a number of goals, was transferred back to Bradford two years later, and never truly realised his potential. However, Bremner met up with him again at the start of the 1969/70 season, when McCole appeared at the hotel at which the Leeds players were having a pre-match meal before the opening game at home to Tottenham. 'The gaffer has seen him in the foyer, brought him into the restaurant, and said to the boys: "This is John McCole – he is one of the players who made this club." Most of the boys didn't know who he was, but anyway, the gaffer has invited him to come on the team coach – and during the journey to the ground, John, having had too much to drink – is sick. Actually, he spewed up on Clarkey, who was sitting next to him at the back, but when the gaffer was told of this, he just said: "So what? You look at what that boy's done for this club." He was like that with all the old players. "You wouldn't have a club here if it wasn't for this fella," he'd say.'

In view of this loyalty, Revie's acute sense of responsibility to colleagues, it was hardly surprising that Bremner, and the other Leeds players who came to the fore under his command, would have run through brick walls for them if he had needed them to do so; so much so that, according to Bremner, some of the players' wives felt that Revie had too big an influence on their husbands. In his own case, he reveals: 'Vikky always found it difficult to forgive the gaffer over an incident in 1967, when I was in agony with stomach pains on the Friday night before a match. The doctor and the gaffer both came around, and after the doc had examined me he told the gaffer: "I think it could be appendicitis." The gaffer's first reaction was to say: "Don't tell him," which really angered Vikky because she knew that he had once had the experience of an appendix rupturing. Anyway, they came back up the stairs, and the doctor agreed that it would probably be OK for me to wait until the end of the season before having it removed. So that's what I did.

'It was typical of the gaffer. He could do things like that because the guys loved him – they still love him.' None more so than Bremner, who took Revie's desperate struggle against motor-neurone disease, and his death, worse than anyone.

Revie was not the only person who did much to help shape Bremner's remarkable career. The first was inevitably his father. Born and raised in Stirling, Bremner recalls:

> My father [who spent most of his working years in the army]
> did not know a great deal about the game, but he was
> enthusiastic without being overbearing. You know, the best
> thing my father gave me was my childhood, he never tried to
> live his life again through me. When I see fathers shouting
> and bawling at their sons from the touchline, and the kids
> coming off in tears because they have lost, I think back to my
> father, when I was nine, ten, eleven – he was never like that.
>
> So, while I loved winning, the main thing was that I loved
> playing. Clarkey (Allan Clarke) misses the game desperately
> now, he really does. When we go back to Elland Road, now,
> he'll say: 'I wish I was out there playing,' but I don't. I never
> have done since I stopped playing. I miss the comradeship
> with all the boys, and all that, but as I say to Clarkey: 'You
> always played to your maximum so you shouldn't have any
> regrets.' I think the people who really miss it are the people
> who never really enjoyed it when they had it, people who
> maybe were afraid to express themselves.
>
> People have said to me: 'You must have played hard for
> the manager,' but the answer is yes and no. I played hard for
> me, and for the fans. I was always very conscious of the fans,
> especially when I played away. I used to cast my mind back
> to when I was a kid and went with my dad to watch Scotland
> play. As a punter, I would forgive them anything – except
> not trying. The gaffer put that into our heads at times. You
> know, if we were playing in London, he'd say: 'Look, it's hard
> for some people to get to football matches – it's a lot of money
> – but all they expect from you is commitment.' It comes back
> to my father's point about not cheating myself.
>
> My father wasn't the only person who encouraged me to
> enjoy my football. I also remember a man called Bill Sykes,
> who ran my secondary school [St Modan's High School]
> football team. It was the most successful in Stirlingshire, but
> all he ever said to us was: 'Go and enjoy yourselves, boys. It's
> not the end of the world if you are beaten.'

During that period, when Bremner was 13, he met Alex Smith,
who has forged a successful career in Scotland as a coach and

manager, and who has long been one of Bremner's closest friends and counsellors. Smith, two years older than Bremner, was training with the youth team he played for (Gowanhill Juniors) when Bremner turned up on his bike and asked the manager to give him a game. 'The manager told me to bugger off sort of thing, but Alex intervened: "Oh, give the kid a game," Alex says. "There's no problem with the kid playing." So I started playing for that team, as well as the school side, and Alex took me under his wing. He was brilliant. I really looked up to him – you know, unlike him, I came from a real working-class area and, to someone like me, he was quite sophisticated. You know what he used to do? He had started driving by the time I started playing in the trial matches for Scotland and other representative teams, and he'd ferry me around in his baby Austin. He had a fantastic influence on me, he really did. It was one of the biggest disappointments of my life that Alex, though he has had a good career in football, never made it at the highest levels as a player.'

As for Bremner's success in that department, the paths of Revie and himself crossed in 1959 when Bremner, a year after the then 32-year-old Revie's transfer to Leeds as a player from Sunderland for £12,000, joined the club as a 16-year-old apprentice. It seems strange that Bremner should elect to go to Leeds, given that he was looked upon as one of the most exciting schoolboy players in Britain and had no shortage of top clubs chasing him. 'The club I really wanted to play for was Celtic,' he admits. 'But my father was a Protestant and my mum was a Catholic and my father was sensitive about the religious bigotry in Glasgow, especially with regard to the rivalry between Celtic and Rangers. He kept saying: "Look, it doesn't matter whether you stay here [in Stirling] or stay in Glasgow, you are always going to have this religious thing." I had never heard of Leeds United as such. As a boy, my favourite English team was Exeter City believe it or not. I hadn't a clue where they were situated – they could have been in Australia for all I knew – but I was attracted to them by their

name. I used to think: "Oh, it must be great playing for them."
Anyway, what really clinched the decision to sign for Leeds
was that my father was impressed with Harry Reynolds [the
then Leeds chairman]. My father was quite an astute man, and
after meeting Reynolds, he just says to me: "Nice man." So that
was it.' It was a move that Bremner was to regret, although
any outsider viewing his early progress at Leeds would have
thought that the reverse was true.

In January 1960, Bremner, just turned 17, made his first-
team debut in a 3–1 win at Chelsea, operating at outside right
with Revie giving him the benefit of his know-how at inside
right. The partnership was used in ten more First Division
matches that season, when Leeds dropped into the Second
Division, and Revie and Bremner also played together in seven
matches the following season. However, it was when Revie
became player-manager in March 1961, at a time when Leeds
seemed in danger of slipping into the Third Division, that
Bremner's career took off.

Revie, with no doubt that this precocious youngster
represented his best chance of making a success of his first
managerial job, had to battle hard to keep him at Elland Road.
Leeds were heavily in debt then, and within three months of
his taking over, Revie was told by the board that the club had
received a £25,000 offer for Bremner from Everton, and that
they had decided to accept it. 'He's one of the best players we've
got,' Revie said. 'If you sell him, there is no way this club is
going to go anywhere.' This did not carry much weight with
the directors, who remained adamant about the transfer, so
Revie told them he was quitting and stormed out of the room.
As he was leaving the ground, however, one of the directors
caught up with him and said: 'You can come back upstairs –
we are keeping him.'

Bremner himself, though, was not happy at Leeds. Ever
since joining the club he had been homesick for his native
Scotland, as was a player called Tommy Henderson, a fellow
member of Scotland's 1958 schoolboy team who had come to

Elland Road at the same time. Bremner says: 'In those days, Leeds had more than 50 pros and ran four teams – the youth team, which we were in, the A team, the reserves and the first team – and I made a pact with Tommy that if we didn't get into the reserves by the end of that first season, we would both clear off back home. There seemed no way that either of us was going to get that high up the ladder, but three matches from the end of the season, I bloody get put in the reserves at Preston. So Tommy left, and I stayed on – but I was still homesick. Believe it or not, even when I got married to Vikky [in 1963] I was still homesick.'

Some time before then, Bremner had been approached by the representative of a club in Scotland asking if he would be interested in a move to them. Bremner was enthusiastic about the idea, but when the club approached Leeds, Revie quoted them a transfer fee of £35,000 for him, just £18,000 short of the British record fee that Manchester City had paid Huddersfield for Denis Law. Years later, when Bremner was discussing it with Les Cocker, the Leeds trainer, Cocker told him: 'No matter how much that Scottish club said they would pay for you, the gaffer would have asked for more. There was no way you were going.'

Despite the set-back, Bremner continued to press for a move. In May 1962, in a registered letter to the chairman, he wrote: 'I am very sorry to have to inform you that I cannot settle down, nor in England for that matter. I have tried, believe me I have tried. It is not the club I have any complaints about, but I would prefer to be back home. Believe me, I have given it a lot of thought and I have made up my mind. The best thing is to get a transfer back to Scotland. I would not go to any other English club. As for Mr Revie, well I can't start to tell you of my regard for him, but honestly, it is just impossible for me to stay in England. It is just how I feel, so please, I am begging the board to give me my transfer back to Scotland. I beg of you.'

A few weeks later, however, Leeds went on a tour of

Italy, where Revie switched Bremner from outside right to midfield, a move which enabled him to get more involved in matches. Revie then enlisted the help of two of the people closest to him, Vikky (then Bremner's fiancée) and Alex Smith. From then on, Vikky, inevitably impressed by Revie's initiative in travelling to Scotland to discuss the problem with her, repeatedly encouraged Bremner to concentrate on establishing a successful career at Elland Road. For his part, Smith kept telling Bremner – tongue in cheek – about all the negative aspects of being in Scotland.

By this time, Bremner, who withdrew his transfer request during the early part of the 1962/63 season, had been given another good reason to remain at Leeds – the influence of midfielder Bobby Collins. Revie had bought Collins from Everton for £25,000 just before the transfer deadline in March 1962. At 31, the former Scottish international was regarded as past his best, but it was to prove one of the most astute soccer buys of all time. Collins, conscious of his responsibilities as the elder statesman of the Leeds team, played a major part in lifting them out of relegation trouble that season and back into the First Division in 1964. He was captain of the team when they won the Second Division title in 1964, and the following season his continued new lease of life led to his being named Footballer of the Year and being recalled to the Scotland team after a six-year absence.

During this time, Collins, among the most respected of all post-war professionals, emerged as something of a guru to the young Leeds players, notably to Bremner. It was perhaps inevitable that Bremner should look upon him in this way, and not just because he was at an impressionable age. Collins, even shorter than him at 5ft 4in, had played for Celtic when Bremner watched them as a boy; and Collins, through his tough confrontational streak, was one of the few professionals capable of imposing his will on Bremner. Revie might have been a father-figure to him off the field, but Collins, as mentally and physically strong as any footballer in Britain, came very much into that category.

That he and Bremner were kindred spirits in some ways is summed up by two Revie anecdotes about Collins. One concerns that close season tour of Italy in 1962: 'When we played Roma, he and Jack Charlton had a terrific row at half-time over a mistake by Jack towards the end of the first half. It was so humid that night that, as they were arguing, Jack suddenly decided to take a quick cold shower, but Bobby, who remember was like a midget compared to Jack, tore after him and before we knew what had happened, they were swapping punches. I actually had to dash into the shower cubicle to separate them, ruining a new lightweight suit in the process. But I didn't mind that because at least the incident showed that they cared about their performances.' There was another clash between Collins and Charlton in March 1965. Revie explained:

> The players were taken to a Harrogate hotel on the eve of the home match against Burnley and, upon going to their rooms to turn in for the night, Bobby and Jack became involved in a water-throwing battle. Jack started it by knocking on Bobby's bedroom door and throwing a jug of water over him. Of course, Bobby wasn't going to turn a blind eye to that, was he? He chased Jack down the corridor to get his own back – and put his right arm through a glass door. He had to be rushed to hospital and the wound needed 16 stitches. Now, I had spent the evening at a local referees' society meeting and didn't learn of the accident until the players arrived at the ground the next day, a few hours before the kick-off. I gave Bobby a dressing down, arranged for one of our young players to take his place in the team, and went into my office to try and cool down. But in came Bobby, pleading with me to let him play. No substitutes were allowed in those days, so my first reaction was that it would be taking too much of a chance to use somebody who probably would not last the full 90 minutes. However, I finally gave in and Les Cocker used so much bandage and wadding on Bobby's right arm that it was almost twice the size of his left and impossible for him to bend it. But that night, Bobby played

what I would think was one of the best games of his career. He scored two goals and made two others in a 5–1 win that lifted us to the top of the First Division. When he came into the dressing-room afterwards, he was covered in mud and blood was seeping through the bandage on his arm and dripping onto the floor. But he just grinned at me and said: 'There you are – I told you I wouldn't let you down tonight.' He was a man who hated losing. His attitude rubbed off on everyone else.

Bremner provides an equally glowing appraisal of Collins's influence on the team, and himself. 'He was a great, great captain, he really was. People might find this funny, but he ruled by fear. Now you might think; "He was only 5ft 4in, how could he rule by fear?" But he did. Whatever he said to us, we would jump. Like, if he said we had to do this for ten minutes or that for ten minutes, we would do it. He really was quite frightening at times. People don't appreciate the power that he had over the team. He influenced a lot of the younger guys with regards to the desire to win.'

Collins took the game ultra-seriously. He took himself ultra-seriously, too, occasionally portraying a macho streak that could be directed even against his own players. As Eddie Gray recalls: 'When he played for the ex-Leeds players' side in charity matches, he was still having kicks at people at the age of 65. Unbelievable – he's 65, and he still wants to fight people. As captain of the team in the 1960s, his competitiveness in training had to be seen to be believed. As soon as you saw that little finger go up, pointing at someone, you knew the person was in trouble. It was great, you know? I mean, some of the clashes that took place in training between Bobby and Billy . . .'

Bremner nods in agreement. 'I remember we were playing a five-a-side, when the ball was knocked up to me, with Collins behind me,' he says. 'I did not know he was the one marking me, but I managed to sell him a dummy – I shaped to go one way, and as he moved with me, I beat him by turning the other way. The boys started laughing, so the next time I got the ball, Bobby came in with a tackle that nearly killed me. At this point, Les Cocker, who could see there was trouble brewing, called a halt to the game. "That's it, game finished," he said. I said to Norman [Hunter]: "What did I do?" It was Norman who told me that Bob had been the player I had beaten in that incident, and that he'd got upset by the lads laughing over it. Bob would do things like that. You had to watch Bob in training, if he took the needle with you.'

In hindsight, Bremner can see why Collins' influence on him might not have been entirely positive. Referring to the period in his career when he repeatedly landed in trouble with referees, he says: 'When they see me now, the supporters of other teams say: "Aye, you were a dirty wee so and so." They are surprised when I tell them that I was only sent off about three times. But I was booked loads of times. It's hard to put your finger on it. I mean, I was very passionate. All the lads were passionate together, as a unit, but I was the most fiery one. I used to go crazy when someone kicked one of our boys, I got upset by referees ... but, you know, I honestly can't remember being like that before Bobby came. I've spoken with Vikky about this and she says: "You must have been." But when I played for Scotland schoolboys, and in my first couple of years in Leeds's first team, I can't remember having goes at people and things like that.'

It was inevitable, perhaps, that Bremner would become less explosive as he got older and more mature. Two other factors that helped him exploit his natural aggression and competitiveness, in a less self-destructive manner were sparked, ironically, by Collins's misfortune in breaking a leg in a European Fairs Cup tie against Torino in Italy in October 1965. It led to Bremner taking over from Collins as Leeds captain, and John Giles, who had been signed from Manchester United as a right winger two years earlier, succeeding Collins as the team's midfield general. Nowadays, when talking about the brilliance of the Leeds midfield when Bremner and Giles were at the hub of it, it is impossible to mention one player without the other. From the mid-1960s to the mid-1970s, the pair's rapport in the engine room of the awesome Leeds football machine was one of the most highly acclaimed in the history of the game. To watch the pair in action was to witness midfield play at its most exciting, technically sophisticated level. Giles, only slightly taller than Bremner at 5ft 7in, was a brilliant passer of the ball with either foot. Moreover, the Dublin-born Giles, who gained 60 Irish Republic caps over an international career spanning 19 years (he later became national team manager), was as thoughtful and studious as Bremner was impulsive and excitable. It might be an over-simplification to say that Giles played with his head rather than his heart, while Bremner did it the other way round, but nonetheless, this was the essence of their partnership. 'John was the controller of our play, like the conductor of an orchestra,' Peter Lorimer says. Bremner does not disagree, particularly on the subject of how he personally benefited from Giles's midfield presence:

> Bobby was a marvellous footballer but John was a world-class one. There was nothing John lacked, but the thing that really stood out in his game was his passing. Whether it was short, long, right foot, left foot – it made no difference to him. We seemed to complement each other right from the start. People say to me, even coaches, that we must have worked very hard on our partnership, but we didn't really. We weren't even great buddies. We were pals, but my big buddies were Jack Charlton and Allan Clarke. The thing was, when we were on the park, you would have thought that we were all blood brothers, let alone friends. This was what really got to other teams. On Scotland trips, players would come up to me and say: 'We can't believe you lot at Leeds, Billy. If I kick you, I hear Giles shouting that he will get me, then Norman shouting that he wants to do it, then Paul [Reaney] shouting that they should leave it to him – it's never ending. We have one or two guys who will back

you up in these situations, but we're not like you. Whenever there is an incident with your lot, you are all in it together.' It was the same when you got the ball – you got information from everywhere. If someone had a ball knocked into him and there wasn't an opponent near him, he'd hear someone shout: 'Hold it. Time – you've got time.' Or 'Man on,' or 'Here, here, here.' Whenever you got the ball, you were getting calls to help you.

The communication between Bremner and Giles was particularly important. Bremner was like a firecracker, attracting the ball and opponents to him like a magnet; with Giles taking up excellent positions to take the ball from him when he landed in difficulties. 'You could be 2–0 down, but Gilesey would still not be panicking. Me, I'd be panicking like crazy. Gilesey was the one who would usually drop deep and "show" for short balls from the back four. There can't be two of you doing that, so my job with the team was to support Gilesey in midfield, but also to get up and support Clarkey.

'If we were in trouble, I was always the desperate one, the one who would want to throw caution to the wind and try to retrieve the situation right away. But Gilesey would say: "No, keep playing normally, keep passing, and it will come." '

All of which explains why Leeds under Revie dominated so many matches. Indeed, the brilliance of Bremner and Giles together, and Revie's barely concealed affection for them, led to the manager deliberately finding fault with them during team meetings. Bremner recalls: 'We had a team meeting each Monday, and he'd nearly always start it by criticising the two of us. When I complained about this once to Les Cocker, Les says: "He does it because you two tend to do the best, and he thinks that if he shows the players that he is prepared to get stuck into you, they will have to sit up and take notice of the criticisms he makes of them. So you just sit back and take it." It was crazy at times. Gilesey and I might have played out of our skins on the Saturday, but on the Monday, it would be: "Wee man [Bremner], I can't remember the last time you

120

made a tackle, it must have been months and months ago. John [Giles], you were effing dancing here on the ball, dancing there on the ball . . . you two have really got to get your act together, you really have." We'd come away from the meeting thinking: "What the hell does he want?" '

Revie's sensitivity about being seen to get too carried away by his team's performances, his determination to keep Bremner and Co on their toes, was often illustrated by his apparent low-key reaction, at least publicly, to some of their greatest moments. Leeds hit what many considered to be football perfection during that period in the 1971/72 season, when they hammered Manchester United 5–1 at home on 19 February – another match in which Bremner was at his inspiring best – and then humiliated Southampton at Elland Road the following week. But, looking at Revie's disdainful expression as he watched these thrilling exhibitions, few would have guessed it. Bremner found it even harder to get a more complimentary reaction during Leeds's blistering start to the 1973/74 season: 'He picked on Gilesey and I more than ever,' Bremner says. 'I mean, we had gone ten or 15 matches unbeaten, and he's giving us stick and talking about getting the cheque-book out. That was his favourite theme: "I'm getting the cheque-book out, I have to get the cheque-book out."'

'Obviously, he knew us like the back of his hand, didn't he?' The point brings him back to the memory of Revie criticising him over his tackling. 'The following Saturday, I got in this early tackle that even Jack and Norman would have been proud of, and then looked over to the touchline bench to try and catch the gaffer's eye and maybe give a wee gesture. But he was having none of it, was he? The moment I looked across, he turned his head away, making out as if something had caught his attention behind him. Yeah, yeah, he knew us like the back of his hand.'

Nowadays, Bremner, who ended his playing career with Hull and then had spells as manager of Doncaster Rovers and Leeds (where he succeeded Eddie Gray), is no longer directly involved with football; he earns his living through media work and after-dinner speaking. It seems a pity that the Leeds fans can't see more of him in action in charity matches, but the Leeds United ex-players association team is run by Lorimer, who says he has misgivings about whether his old friend and colleague is strong enough, physically, for such games. 'Billy's legs have gone,' Lorimer claims, with a mischievous smile. 'I know that I have put on a lot of weight since my retirement from the game, but I can easily take it off. As for Billy, you look at his legs – there are no muscles there.'

No doubt, in view of the fact that Bremner's heart is still as big as it was, and that you never lose the technical skill with which you are born, Lorimer's comments will prove beneficial to his team when he needs to call on Bremner to prove him wrong. Bremner says: 'My father always used to say to me: "You can get away with cheating other people, but you can't get away with cheating yourself. Never cheat yourself." '

This philosophy became Bremner's trademark. It brought him 150 Leeds goals in all, but perhaps the one that best epitomised the indomitable spirit of the man was that header – yes, header – that enabled their then raw young team to reach the 1965 FA Cup final at Manchester United's expense. It was a season in which Leeds had been constantly in the news, and not just because of their results. In the August issue of *FA News*, the Football Association's official magazine, they were labelled the roughest team in England, a tag based on the fact that during their 1963/64 promotion season they had collected the highest number of bookings – 18 – in the country. This was somewhat misleading, as most of the cautions had been meted out to their junior players, and there was no mention of the fact that Leeds did not have one player sent off during the period in question, while Manchester United had five. However, the image of Leeds as a team who could seriously damage your health escalated, with opposing sides – and supporters – hyping themselves up for a brutal physical battle even before a ball had been kicked, and Leeds, fuelled by a strong siege mentality, became increasingly belligerent.

The most disturbing example of the atmosphere this created was the league match at Everton on 7 November 1964, when the mood of the fans, and players, became so ugly that the referee, Ken Stokes, stopped the game and took the teams off the field for ten minutes to allow everyone to cool down. Leeds won 1–0, but it was Everton who came out on top in the foul count, committing 19 against Leeds's 13. Leeds also faced Everton at Goodison in the FA Cup, beating them 2–1 in the fourth round after a 1–1 draw at Elland Road.

Those were the only goals Leeds conceded on their journey to Wembley, having beaten Southport 3–0 in the third round, Shrewsbury (2–0) and Crystal Palace (3–0). The Palace tie was another game which reflected Leeds's macho image, and how it influenced the approach of other sides in matches against them. On the day of the game, Palace's manager, Dick Graham, showed his players a video of one of Leeds's physical games, and told them: 'That there is the hardest team in Britain – until tonight. Tonight, you are going to be the hardest team in Britain. If I see any of you pulling out of a tackle, you will never play for this club again.' In the first half, Palace, indeed, challenged for the ball as if their very lives depended on winning it. Jim Storrie, then playing up front for Leeds, recalled: 'They were kicking everything that moved. Eventually, when someone went down injured and was having treatment, wee Billy ambled up to their captain, John Sewell, and said: "I don't think that what you lot are doing is a good idea." Sewell said: "What do you mean?" and Billy said: "Well, if the score stays at 0–0, just think of what we will do to your lot in the replay at our place." According to Billy, you could see by the look in Sewell's eyes that he'd got the message.'

If regular Leeds-watchers had winced at the ferocity of the action against Everton and Palace, one wonders what they will have thought of the Leeds–Manchester United semi-final battles. The violence in the goalless draw at Hillsborough resulted in no fewer than 34 fouls, 24 by United. For the replay at the City Ground, Nottingham, two days later, Revie switched his attacking left-back, Terry Cooper, to outside left, in a defensive role. The logic behind this was that in the previous match Pat Crerand had been at the hub of virtually every United attack, and Revie reasoned that if Cooper came in-field to mark him, it would have the effect of stopping the supply of passes to him. However, with Bobby Charlton and Denis Law rising to the occasion, United gradually adjusted to this. In the second half, Leeds hovered on the brink of defeat as United stretched their defence with a number of cunning attacking moves. Goalkeeper Gary Sprake was the Leeds hero during this critical period, making world-class saves from Law and Charlton and repeatedly cutting out dangerous crosses with the Leeds defence spreadeagled.

But with 20 minutes to go, and Leeds looking unlikely to weather the storm for much longer, Bremner moved forward into the attack and Giles switched from outside right to support Collins in midfield. Seventeen minutes later, Giles and Bremner combined to score the only goal. It came from a free-kick for a foul on Collins by Stiles, ironically Giles's brother-in-law. Bremner says: 'Gilesey was ready to take the kick, and although I joined the others in the penalty area, by the far post area, I thought: "There's no way he's going to put it anywhere near me – he'll try and hit big Jack." So Gilesey hits this ball, and it is coming towards me. I've got my back to the goal, and I am thinking that any second the goalkeeper is going to come and splatter me. The ball was just drifting beyond me, so knowing that I wasn't tall enough to direct it properly, all I tried to do was just get my head to it and divert it back across the goal. But, having caught it with the top of my head, it flew into the top corner of the net.'

Lucky? Maybe, but then Bremner, whose enthusiasm for the game, and ambitions, knew no bounds, made his own luck.

Like a number of the Leeds players of that golden Elland Road era, he finds it difficult to pinpoint the match which gave him the most satisfaction. 'It is a hard question, because the boys were so consistent,' he explains. 'The gaffer used to say to us: "I don't want fly-by-nights who will give me two good games out of ten. I expect my players to give me maybe seven games when they are at or near their peak, and the other three so-so." ' He finds it easier to remember his worst matches – i.e. the 1965 FA Cup final against Liverpool. 'I can accept defeat when I know that we have played not bad and that the other team have had the luck on the day, but we froze against Liverpool that day. They were much more experienced than us and much the better team. Some of the lads did OK, but although I scored, I was rubbish.'

But mostly, Bremner was outstanding, and never more so than when he produced that 'doddle' of a performance in the sweeper role against Hibernian in 1974. Leeds were knocked out by Portugal's Vitoria Setúbal in the next UEFA Cup round, but with Bremner in that sort of form, it was hardly surprising that Leeds won the Championship for the second time – in a manner which could also have been described as a 'doddle'.

8

John Giles

John Giles played 524 first-team matches for Leeds in his 12 years with the club (1963–1975), and in very few of them was he singled out as the star performer by the fans and the media. One exception concerned a match at Chelsea, where his high number of subtle touches on the ball, the countless unspectacular yet intelligent passes that enabled him to control the pattern of the game, led Ken Jones to suggest in the *Daily Mirror* that he could have played Chelsea on his own. Pass the ball, get it back; pass, get it back ... to keep your eye on Giles for the entire 90 minutes was to invite the feeling that his football was hypnotic. Jones, a former professional footballer and coach, and thus a man well-equipped to appreciate the finer technical points of the game, said that Giles did not need his nine outfield team-mates; all he needed was ten strategically placed benches.

But this glowing praise for a master craftsman at work was rare for Giles. He says that the performance that gave him the most satisfaction and pride was against Liverpool in the UEFA Cup (then called the Inter Cities Fairs Cup) semi-final first leg at Anfield on 13 April 1971. Significantly, though, the only reference to him in the local newspaper report of the game concerns the fact that he 'worked hard' in midfield and that it was from his free-kick that Billy Bremner headed the only goal. As always, it was Bremner, the more dynamic of the two – and back in the side, as a striker, after a three-month absence – who attracted the most media attention.

Giles, too, scored goals – he got 151 for Leeds. But the significance of his contribution in the tight midfield battles, a contribution invariably as understated as this quietly spoken charming Irishman himself, tended to be lost on many fans. So, if they weren't raving about Bremner, they were raving about Eddie Gray, or Peter Lorimer, or Allan Clarke. Meanwhile, though, most managers, coaches and players in Britain – including his fellow proessionals at Leeds, were raving about John Giles. To them, Giles was the brains of the Leeds team, the man who did the most to dictate the tempo and nature of their play. When a Leeds defender gained possession deep in his own half, Giles was usually the first player to receive it and set their attack in motion; and wherever the ball was played from then on, Giles would be available to take it back and redirect operations. Bremner might have been the Leeds orchestra's outstanding soloist, but Giles held the conductor's baton.

It was rare that Giles was happy with all that he did with it because he was a perfectionist. If he had been a professional golfer, one suspects that a course with floodlights on the practice ground would have kept him there all night. As it is, Giles has become more attached to golf than ever since his retirement from football and it is a standing joke among his friends that his local club is virtually his second home. It is typical of him that, though now down to a four handicap, it clearly frustrates him that no matter how much work he puts into his game, this is as far as he is liable to go. But the one thing which does not frustrate him is that so much of his work with a football went unnoticed, or not fully appreciated, by the general public. All players like praise, but in Giles's case the praise he got from his fellow professionals, combined with the satisfaction of knowing himself that he had at least tried to do everything in the proper manner, was all he ever wanted.

The 'Gentle Giant', John Charles – the best loved of the pre-Revie stars

ABOVE: One of the most nerve-wracking sights for any goalkeeper: Peter 'Hot Shot' Lorimer pulls back that lethal right foot for a shot

RIGHT: The late Don Revie, one of the all-time great British managers

FAR RIGHT: The underrated but ultra-effective full-back Paul Reaney. Effective? Just ask George Best

ABOVE: A Liverpool player, preparing to do battle with Norman Hunter (right), invites speculation that he has a death wish

LEFT: The human goalscoring machine called Allan 'Sniffer' Clarke

RIGHT: The conductor of the Leeds
orchestra, John Giles

BELOW: His irrepressible midfield partner –
and the club's greatest captain –
Billy Bremner

ABOVE: Gordon Strachan, the best of the post-Revie stars

RIGHT: Lee Chapman. No Eric Cantona or Tony Yeboah – but look at his scoring record

EFT: Eddie Gray, the winger whose FA Cup nal show at Wembley was comparable to hat of even Stan Matthews

John Lukic – Mr Unflappable

Emotional he wasn't. As he says: 'I was never a crowd pleaser, in the sense of having a great relationship with the crowd. People come to see you play because you can do things that they can't; you are supposed to do those things, and you do them. That's why I can never understand why some players applaud the crowd. I would never do that – they should be clapping you.

'I played 12 years at Leeds, and I don't think I was ever in the top three in the supporters' Player of the Year polls – that's not a gripe, it's a fact. Now, it would have been nice had I got more recognition from them, but it honestly didn't bother me that I didn't. You see, the thing I wanted more than anything else from football was the respect of the people I played with and against, but mostly the people I played with.' For Giles, that meant showing the moral courage to keep taking responsibility, to keep putting himself into situations for the good of the team, as opposed to situations that would make him look good in the eyes of the crowd.

'To be able to come off the field thinking: "Well, I didn't have a good game, but at least I didn't bottle it," ' he adds.

One telling example of this is Giles's record as Leeds's penalty taker: he took around 50 for them and missed no more than three. Another illustration was provided by Leeds's shock defeat at the hands of the then Second Division Sunderland in 1973. Giles was pressured into a mistake by a Sunderland player when moving deep into the Leeds penalty area to receive a throw-out from goalkeeper David Harvey, an error from which Leeds were fortunate not to go 2–0 down. A couple of minutes later, however, Giles had the Leeds fans' hearts in their mouths by doing it again.

> All you have to do [to avoid the possibility of looking an indifferent player] is to take just two or three steps the wrong way, and you don't get the ball and you don't make mistakes. Now the crowd wouldn't notice it, but your fellow players would notice it. If you had that mentality, then in the supporters' eyes you would never have a bad game. I never

came out of a game 100 per cent happy with my performance
– there wasn't one match where I could say there wasn't one
thing about my performance that nagged me. But whether
I played well or badly, I always tried to do the things that
needed to be done. You were true to yourself, that was
the thing.

To be able to do that, it was important to switch off from the
crowd. The main thing in football is to keep your head all the
time, not got get too excited when you are up or too low when
you are down. You have to be dispassionate. If you're winning
1–0 after 20 minutes, but playing a lot of rubbish, the crowd
would live with that. But if you were a goal down, but playing
well, then they would moan and groan. In that situation, they
would hate it when they saw me coming deep to get the ball.
Their attitude was: 'Get up the pitch – what are you doing
back there?' But you knew it was the right thing to do.

I did not get the joy from it that other people – supporters
– might have thought I got. I got my enjoyment for different
reasons. When people watch matches, they tune in to the
glamour and they think: 'Oh, I wish I could be out there –
I wish it could be me scoring that goal.' But when it's your
profession, it's a different type of enjoyment. For example,
though spectators might have got a buzz out of seeing me hit
a great pass, I didn't because I had the ability to do it and I
was expected to do it. I took it for granted. Instead of getting
a buzz out of it, I was more likely to end up disappointed over
not being able to do it every time. So it's satisfaction rather
than enjoyment, your own personal satisfaction in knowing
that you did your job.

The basic terms of reference of Giles's job were to dictate the
play. Creating and scoring goals might have been the essential
end-product of that, but to Giles, this had to be combined
with the aim of not giving the ball away unnecessarily.
Occasionally, it was argued that he took this to the extreme,
but he says: 'To say that I didn't play enough chancy balls
sometimes because I didn't want to give the ball away would
be an over-simplification of it. It was a question of whether
I thought it was the right ball to hit, or whether I was able
to see that it was the right ball to hit. Yes, there were times

when I played the simple pass when, if I'd have looked up a bit more quickly, I could have played a more penetrative one. But people who are watching a game can see a lot more than people who are playing in it. I have heard people say that I wanted to play "perfect" football all the time. I'm not sure what they mean by that, but if they mean doing the right things at the right times, well, doesn't everyone want to play perfect football?'

So now you know why Giles's presence made Don Revie's Leeds the perfect team, much to the chagrin of Manchester United. Giles's brilliance at Leeds was a sore point with United, of course, because they signed the Dubliner from Home Farm in November 1957, when he was 17, and let him go to Leeds for £33,000 six years later, shortly after he helped them win the FA Cup. Giles, who had joined United as an inside forward but played around half of his matches for them at outside right due to the high number of quality players available for the midfield spots, had not been happy at Old Trafford for some time. In fairness to United, Giles himself wanted to leave. It was widely assumed that he asked for a transfer as a result of being dropped from the first team for the opening First Division match of the season, following United's 4–0 defeat by Everton in the Charity Shield. But in his autobiography, he explained: 'This was merely the sequel to many months of friction between the club and myself.'

He traced it back to April 1962, when United were beaten 3–1 by Spurs in the FA Cup semi-final. He played in midfield that day (he was at inside right, with Bobby Charlton at inside left) and he recalled:

> I had a nightmare. I hardly put a ball right all afternoon and repeatedly lost possession. None of the United players played well, but my errors stood out more because I was supposed to be the 'general' of the team. Frankly, I don't think the club ever forgave me for that performance. This might seem an exaggeration, but looking back, I find it significant that hardly a week went by without Matt Busby or Jimmy Murphy

finding some fault with my game. I consider there were times when their criticism was harsh to say the least. I became more and more despondent, and it didn't help when I learned I was being criticised behind my back. Each Sunday, the coaching staff had a meeting to discuss the club's results at all levels the previous day. When I arrived at the club on the Monday morning, someone like Wilf McGuiness [then the reserve team trainer] would invariably make a comment such as: 'See you had another disappointing game on Saturday.' Perhaps I was over-sensitive and immature, but these comments did hurt and caused me to mistrust Busby and Murphy. I am not denying that they are among the best managers in the game – their record underlines this beyond doubt. It is just that I personally lost faith in them because I got the impression of their not having any faith in me.'

The other factor which Giles said made him feel insecure and disillusioned at Old Trafford was that 'there was not a good team spirit there at the time'. United had struggled in the League in that FA Cup-winning season, and Giles argued: 'We were unfortunate in getting off to a disappointing start to the season, which resulted in the players losing confidence and directing their frustration at each other. I doubt very much if this would have happened had there been more "home-grown" players in the side. One of the greatest attributes of the pre-Munich Manchester United team was their sense of unity. Most of the players had virtually grown up together, having progressed through the club's youth and reserve teams, and were like brothers. However, in the five years after the Munich disaster the team became much more cosmopolitan. The side which started the season, with big money signings like Albert Quixall, David Herd, Noel Cantwell, Maurice Setters, Denis Law and Pat Crerand, was a good side on paper, full of individual flair and experience. Unfortunately, however, the potential was undermined by a clash of personalities.'

Despite all this, the basic truth about Giles's inability to realise his potential at Manchester United is that at that stage of his career and, more pertinently, his development as a person, it was the wrong club at the wrong time for him. Giles recalls that when United agreed to his transfer request, McGuiness deemed it necessary to try and 'console' him. 'Don't worry, John,' he said. 'Maybe Busby will change his mind.' McGuiness might well have been ready to send Giles a condolence card when Leeds signed him, given that they were in the Second Division. But Giles recalls: 'They had made a great run from Christmas the previous season, they only just missed promotion, so I knew there was something happening there. I didn't join them just for the sake of getting another job. For me, it is better to go to a club that is trying to do something in the Second Division, than some nuthouse in the First. There was a tremendous sense of ambition at Leeds and I was fortunate to be part of that.'

Leeds, indeed, were ready to launch themselves to the top under the inspiring leadership of Don Revie off the field and Bobby Collins on it; and Leeds, through the closely-knit one-for-all-all-for-one family spirit that Revie had begun to instil into his success-hungry troops, were able to provide the perfect environment for this somewhat inhibited young Irishman to blossom. That season, Leeds won the Second Division Championship, although Giles did not start it with the flourish that might have been expected. His first impression of his new team, in a 3–0 home win over Bury, was that they relied too heavily on running power and lacked the composure to gain the edge over more experienced rivals like Sunderland, Newcastle, Middlesbrough and Preston.

As for his own form, it was so erratic in the first six months that Revie dropped him for the clash with Southampton at Elland Road in March. Giles, who concedes that he did much to bring this situation upon himself through continuing to live in Manchester for four months after his transfer ('The journey to Leeds for training rarely took me less than two hours'), said that he felt he had reached 'rock bottom'. But that blow stung him into greater effort. 'I had visions of everyone at Manchester United laughing at me, and thinking: "Serves him right for thinking that he could do better for himself away from Old Trafford." So being dropped by Leeds was probably the best thing that could have happened to me.' Indeed, Giles was back in the side for the next match, scored one of their goals in a 3-1 win over promotion rivals Middlesbrough, and from that point, never looked back.

The other experience that could be described as being the best thing that could have happened to him was rubbing shoulders with Collins. Giles is by no means the only Leeds player on whom Collins had a major influence; indeed, all the men who played with him at Leeds wax lyrical on how much they learned from him. But Collins's influence on Giles, during a period when Giles was developing the mental toughness that was eventually to see him switched from outside right to Collins's play-maker role in the centre of midfield, was particularly profound. 'You have to be fairly mature to be able to do that job,' he says. 'I was only 21 when I did it at Manchester United in the semi-final against Spurs, and wasn't as mature or experienced as I needed to be. But at 25, and after playing three years with Bobby, I was ready for it.' Mental toughness? Giles explains: 'Bobby was a great player – he had a great attitude to the game. Now, people would say that this applies to every footballer but they don't understand. There's attitudes and attitudes. Bobby's will to win was much stronger than it is in a lot of other cases. He was also more positive. I've often related instances where Leeds would have a couple of first-team players out, and we'd be sitting in the dressing-room before the match thinking: "Oh, things look really dodgy for us today." But I don't think the thought of us not winning ever crossed his mind.'

That mental toughness also encompassed a determination not to be pushed around, a willingness to impose himself on a game physically as well as technically. Collins, though one of the smallest players in the Football League, was also one of the most combative. This was another area in which Giles – 5ft 7in and 10 stone – learned from him. Giles says that

134

he'd been able to 'take care of myself' for some time; since the November day in 1962, in fact, when a bad tackle by an opponent in a Manchester United match at Birmingham left him with badly damaged left ankle ligaments and put him out of action for four months. The operation he underwent was so delicate that the surgeon who conducted it later told him: 'I did not think you had more than a fifty-fifty chance of playing top-class professional football again.' Despite Giles's recovery, the experience proved to him that, if he was ever to fulfil his potential, he would need to be prepared to take the law into his own hands. 'I thought: "Relying on the referee for protection is not going to work. I'm going to have to get stuck in." I was well able to do it before, but I didn't think it was necessary. When I got clogged at Birmingham, my attitude changed.'

Any doubts he might have had concerning the wisdom of going down this road with Leeds were dispelled by the example set by Collins. Inevitably, there were times when Giles became over-sensitive about not being seen to be easily intimidated, giving out greater 'stick' than he received. One Leeds player who took exception to this was Jack Charlton, who once complained angrily to Giles, and Don Revie, about 'some of the wee man's challenges'. 'Big Jack didn't want any hassle,' Giles says. 'If I started any hassle, then he felt that the big centre-forward he was marking might get a bit aggressive or whatever towards him and make his own job more difficult.' Giles was unmoved. 'Well, Jack,' he'd say, matter-of-factly, 'you should just be pleased that I am playing with you, not against you.' Billy Bremner laughed over this ultra-strong self-preservation streak in Giles. 'He probably commits more fouls than I do,' Bremner once remarked. 'But because I am not as calculating as him, I am the one who gets into the most trouble.'

Giles, indeed, was sent off only once in his career, in the first leg of the Fairs Cup semi-final against Real Zaragoza in 1966; and even then, he managed to escape disciplinary action. He had been penalised for a foul on a Zaragoza defender, who then retaliated by punching him on the neck and was also sent off.

On the premise that Giles had been more sinned against than sinning, Leeds asked for a personal hearing; but by the time the case was due to come up, the referee had retired from the game and UEFA had no option but to expunge the incident from their records.

However, Giles was happy that, while the public might not have immediately recognised him as one of the game's 'hard men', his fellow professionals did. He says:

> You had to establish a reputation that would make people think twice about messing with you. I always felt that Bobby sometimes created a bit more space just because of that, because people were quite wary of him. I have certainly done things on a football field that I am embarrassed by now, but one has to put them into the context of the football climate of the times. It was a different game then, much more physical, vicious even, than it is today. But in my time, players like Bobby Collins and myself were targets, right? Before teams went out to play against us, the first thing they'd say in the dressing-room was: 'Look, get hold of these guys. Get stuck into them. Put them out of the game.' Now, you either took that or you responded to it, and Bobby and I certainly responded to it. Nothing would have suited us better than for everybody to go out and play fair, to give us space and not try to kick us. But it didn't happen that way, and you had to get respect in the sense that people could not kick you without knowing they were going to get something back. People might say: 'That wasn't right – that's not sportsmanship.' But that's the way it was, a fact of life.

From the day Giles joined Leeds, it had always been his ambition to succeed Collins as their midfield general. Though Don Revie never told Giles this was what he had in mind for him, Giles took it for granted. However, after Collins suffered a fractured thigh in the European Fairs Cup tie against Torino in October 1965 – Leeds's second season back in the First Division – Giles was 'bitterly disappointed' to find himself still operating at outside right. Rod Johnson, a youngster who had made only a handful of first-team appearances, was drafted into Collins's inside left spot for the First Division clash at Sheffield Wednesday four days later, and kept his place for the following game against West Bromwich Albion in the League Cup. With Leeds having drawn the first game 0–0, and lost the second 4–2, Giles, having brooded over the matter for a few days, arranged for a meeting with Revie to discuss it. But the meeting lasted no more than 30 seconds. As Giles entered Revie's office, the manager just smiled and said: 'I know what you have come in to see me about, John. You'll be pleased to know that you'll be playing at inside forward on Saturday [against Northampton at Elland Road].'

Giles recalls: 'I don't think I have ever been more determined to put on a good show in a match than I was in that one.' Not surprisingly, Leeds won 6–1. Moreoever, as if to prove that their success the previous season had been no fluke, they went on to finish Championship runners-up again, and marked their first-ever tilt at a European trophy by reaching the Fairs Cup final.

And Giles went on to become one of the most distinguished midfield generals in British post-war football history. He did not have a lot of pace, but was quick enough over ten yards to be comfortable when going past opponents with the ball. 'When you are playing in midfield, I think you have to be able to threaten like that,' he says. 'It's very important – if you can beat a player, then everything opens up for you.' But it was the manner in which Giles beat people through his first touch, his passing and his football intelligence that really made him special – that and his desire to keep himself involved in the play. 'My attitude to football was that if you have a lot of ability, if you can control the ball and pass it well, then you should try and get on the ball as much as you can. To be able to have an influence on the play, you couldn't just hit the ball and then stay out of the next stages. I was lucky, in that I wasn't scared of getting the ball in any position. Whatever position I was in, I never thought I would give the ball away.'

It made sense to Giles, and to most others, to be in at the start of Leeds's attacking build-up play, to come deep and make himself available for short passes from his back four players. This occasionally irritated centre-half Jack Charlton, who felt that he was a good enough footballer to be trusted with the responsibility of making a good pass into Leeds's attacking areas and, indeed, would gesture at Giles to move up the field.

During a post-match debate between Giles and Charlton over this, the latter brought Revie into the argument. 'I can do what Gilesey does, can't I?' he proclaimed. 'No, you can't, Jack,' Revie replied.

There were few players in Britain, if any, who could. That Giles was able to use his left foot as effectively as his 'natural' right, thanks to countless hours of practice with his weaker left foot as a boy, was inevitably a major advantage, especially when opposing teams assigned someone to mark him man for man. In such circumstances, the tendency of markers to try and force their opponents to use the foot with which they were less effective was less of a handicap to Giles than it was to most other players of his importance to a team. Many players become frustrated when denied the scope to settle on the ball and fully express their creative talents, but Giles relished the challenge. 'Even if you can't get on the ball as much as you would wish, you can still contribute,' he says, referring to his ability, and his willingness, to make runs off the ball that would create space for others to exploit. 'Different players and teams posed different problems, and you had to be able to improvise. That's one of the things that attracted me to football when I was a kid [when Gaelic football was the main sport in Irish Republic schools]. People talk about strength and fitness in football, but that's only one aspect of it. The real attraction of football to me was to be able to use my imagination and wit, to be able to improvise.'

Quite apart from his own ability, Giles owed much to being part of a machine in which all the parts complemented one another perfectly. Of his famous midfield partnership with

Bremner, he says: 'Billy might have said that I played it a little bit too safe, and I might have said that he was a little bit too adventurous, but we balanced each other. He was inclined to get more forward than I did. He was more dangerous than me in or around the box – he was more liable to beat somebody, or do the unexpected, whereas I would be the one to initiate the move that got Billy into that position. We were quite close to each other in our positioning because, in our own ways, we tried to dominate games and so we were both around the ball. We fed off each other – you know, we'd get into tight areas and to get out of them, we'd be playing little one-twos and things like that. We didn't practise these things in training, we just related to each other naturally.

'All the Leeds players related to each other,' he adds. 'We made it easier for each of us to play to our strengths. For example Norman was a great winner of the ball, a great defender, and when he gained possession, the onus was on me to be close enough to him to ensure that he didn't have to play a long pass or do what I could do with the ball. People like Mick Jones and Eddie Gray would then get into positions to do what they were good at, and so on. That's probably over-simplifying it, but basically Leeds were all about good players each doing what he needed to do.' Equally stimulating to Giles, following the dressing-room back-biting he had experienced at Manchester United, was the extent to which the players bonded emotionally and psychologically. 'We had a few players who were quite mild mannered. I mean, Paul Madeley couldn't kick anybody; nor could Mick Jones and Eddie Gray. But the people who could look after themselves would never allow anybody to take advantage of them. We were very open with each other. If someone had a criticism about someone, it would be voiced openly, not behind the person's back. We could say anything to each other, knowing that it would be taken in the right way, knowing that it had been said for the benefit of the team. Norman Hunter would never say: "Well, it would help me if Terry Cooper [the Leeds full-back on his side of the field] pulled into this position or that position." If he had a point to make about Terry's play, it would be in the context of helping the team.'

Some were less self-centred than others. 'Jack was a strong character who would be inclined to see everything through his own eyes,' Giles acknowledges. 'But we knew that, we understood it, and as a group of people, you just get on with it. You accommodate it. The thing was, when Jack played, he played. Although he probably had different ideas on the game to the rest of us, the bottom line was that he wanted to do well and he wanted to win. He did his stuff.

'Don created the atmosphere for that. Nothing was too much trouble for him. His attention to detail, his discipline, his dedication conveyed itself to the players. People talk about money in the game, but you couldn't put a price on what we had at Leeds. Money wasn't the driving force when I came into the game; it was the personal satisfaction of playing with great players, with the right attitude. That's what I got at Leeds. There were other great teams around during my playing career, Tottenham's double-winning team and the Manchester City team including Mike Summerbee, Colin Bell and Francis Lee, for example. But they were at the top for only three or four years, whereas Leeds were going strong, with basically the same set of players, for more than ten years.'

In that respect, the period which gave him the most satisfaction was in 1973, after Leeds had suffered the humiliation of losing to Sunderland in the FA Cup final. Outside Elland Road, the defeat provoked a strong feeling that Leeds had gone over the hill. The reaction of the Leeds players was rather different. Giles says: 'We blamed ourselves collectively, because we hadn't played well enough as a team, but there was no pointing of fingers at anybody. We just took the stick we got on the chin, and never responded. Our attitude was: "OK, we've had a disappointment, and we've got to get over it and start again." It took a lot of strength of character, but that was what I mean when I talk about the influence of

Don Revie and the atmosphere he created at Leeds.' Leeds opened the 1973/74 season with 29 successive First Division matches without defeat, and went on to win the Championship for the second time. Sunderland, for all the expectation of their triumph over Leeds proving the springboard for a quick return to the top flight, remained in the Second Division.

It was that strength of Leeds character that, following Revie's appointment as England manager in the summer of 1974, enabled Giles and Co to make light of the unsettling effect of having two different managers – Brian Clough and Jimmy Armfield – the following season. Notwithstanding the vastly different manner in which those two men approached the job, it was a particularly unsettling period for Giles – the man that Revie himself had recommended to the Leeds board as his ideal successor. The reasons why they elected to pass up the chance of establishing a measure of management continuity – and went so far in the opposite direction with their controversial choice of a long-time Leeds critic like Clough – has never been fully revealed. What is known is that the Leeds chairman, Manny Cussins, contacted Giles at home to tell him that the board wanted to pursue Revie's idea, but that when Giles arrived at the ground the following morning for his formal interview, Cussins had had a change of mind.

This, some Leeds players believe, was prompted by Bremner also wanting the job, a situation that left Cussins with the fear that selecting one of these key players might alienate the other. To Cussins, choosing an outsider was the best way out of the predicament, but he could hardly have chosen more of an outsider than Clough, whose policy of not showing any respect for Revie's methods and those of the players he'd inherited, was tantamount to his putting a noose around his own neck.

Armfield, the man entrusted with the challenge of steadying the Leeds boat after Clough's stormy 44-day spell at the helm, was somewhat cleverer. He, too, was poles apart from Revie. Quiet and contemplative, the pipe-smoking Armfield gave the impression that he would be far happier playing the organ at his local church – one of his hobbies – than being in charge of such a high-profile and intense band of professionals as those at Elland Road. However, while his apparently laid-back approach could be disconcerting to some players – 'Jimmy's indecision is final,' was the dressing-room in-joke there – it had the effect of encouraging them to take on the responsibility of maintaining the Revie impetus themselves. Giles does not disagree that this in itself was good management by Armfield. Nonetheless, he points out: 'There were so many good players with good professional habits. It was very difficult to mis-manage those lads.'

He himself proved the point by turning a blind eye to a clash with Armfield before the European Champions Cup third-round second-leg tie against Anderlecht in Belgium in March 1974. After a light morning training session on the day of the match, Giles was asked by Peter Lorimer what he felt the Leeds team would be. Leeds had won the first leg 3–0 and Giles named a side that included himself, but not Lorimer and fellow winger, Eddie Gray. 'I think Jimmy will want to play it tight,' he explained. However, when Armfield announced his line-up, Giles was surprised to note that both Lorimer and Gray had been included – and even more so that he wasn't. At this, Giles followed Armfield out of the room, and asked for an explanation. 'Well, the ground's soft,' Armfield told him. 'I don't think the conditions will suit you.' Giles took umbrage at this, pointing out that he'd hardly been hampered by playing in heavy conditions in England. But Giles, one of the Leeds players who was the least enamoured with Armfield's management style, was far too professional to allow this to detract from his performances. It was under Revie, though, that Giles was at his best.

In common with most of the other Leeds stars, he derived particular enjoyment from putting one over on London teams away from home. After all, London was England's media capital, and that was where much of the criticism of Leeds's tactics emanated from. 'It was a bit unfair because the London football writers would generally only see us at places like Tottenham, Arsenal and Chelsea, where our approach was maybe not as attractive as it was when we were playing these sides at home.' One exception to this was that match at Chelsea, when Ken Jones was moved to comment that Giles had virtually played Chelsea on his own. However, Giles himself has mixed feelings about the praise he attracted, on the grounds that it was a match in which neither he nor Leeds were truly stretched. By the same criteria, he dismisses his performances in Leeds's record 10–0 European Cup defeat of the Norwegian amateurs Lyn Oslo on 17 September 1969 – a rout in which he scored two excellent goals – and even the 7–0 destruction of Southampton in 1972. Remind him of the number of passes Leeds strung together at the finish, and he just shrugs and says: 'I would regard it as the least significant of the matches I played in. It was enjoyable for the first 15 minutes or so, while the match was a contest, but after that it was a non-event as far as I was concerned. You get a lot of players who, when their team are winning comfortably, start doing the fancy tricks, the wee flicks and what have you. But, whereas the crowd might remember the exhibition stuff, it means nothing to me. The most enjoyable matches for me are games where you are too busy getting on with your job.'

Leeds's matches against Liverpool came into that category – which brings Giles back to the memory of his display in the 1–0 win at Anfield in the Fairs Cup semi-final in 1971. It was Liverpool's first defeat at Anfield in 12 months, and Giles recalls: 'The two sides were packed with good players. There was pace, there was power, there was skill. Really, there was hardly anything to choose between the two teams and I think I played well. I remember it as one of the matches which summed up what I thought the game should be all about, and which made me feel fulfilled.'

The feeling was maintained when Leeds booked their place in the final with a goalless draw against Liverpool in the second leg, and lifted the trophy for the second time with victory over the Italian giants of Juventus. Of the second leg at Leeds, which ended 1–1, Barry Foster in the *Yorkshire Post*, wrote: 'Giles gave the Italians plenty of problems in midfield, and it was from his promptings that most of Leeds's attacking play developed.' One with particular cause to be grateful for this was the Leeds left-back, Terry Cooper, whose attacking runs down the flanks, many from Giles passes, caused him to stand out even more than Juventus forwards of the calibre of Causio, Anastasi and Bettega.

It was in the arena of European combat, in which Leeds were pitted against teams of a higher technical and tactical calibre than most of those who could be found in the more basic physical environment of the First Division, that Giles's composure and intelligence came in particularly handy. This was certainly true in Leeds's early days in Europe. At the time he joined Leeds, only Collins had previously had any meaningful experience of crossing swords with continental teams. For his part, Giles had played in a number of prestige friendlies against the top teams from other countries during his career at Manchester United, including the one against Real Madrid in 1962 – a testimonial match – when United became the first British side to beat the Spaniards at their Bernabeu Stadium.

Giles's know-how was a major factor in enabling Leeds to settle down and progress at this level of competition much more quickly than most other rookie teams. They followed their unexpected success in reaching the 1966 Fairs Cup final at their first attempt by doing so again the following year. Perhaps their most memorable showing before their ultimate defeat by Dinamo Zagreb came in the third round, when they were held to a 1–1 draw by Valencia at home but beat them 2–0 away. On the night of that second leg, Giles had his mind on other things – the birth of his second child, a daughter, shortly before the kick-off. But it was perhaps typical of him that he should then switch off from that news, and concentrate on destroying Valencia by scoring the first Leeds goal and laying on the second for Lorimer.

Giles, though, is as phlegmatic about the memory of that outstanding performance as he is about all the others. He was 'only' doing his job. He was 'only' doing what was professionally correct.

9

Peter Lorimer

The Nou Camp stadium, the 120,000-capacity home of Barcelona FC, is one of the most imposing and intimidating football theatres in the world. With its steep tiers of seating rising high into the sky, it has the appearance of a gigantic bull-ring, and when Barcelona are at their best, visiting teams are made to feel no different to those animals being set up for the kill.

Leeds United fans must certainly have had that vision when their team faced Barcelona there in the European Champions Cup semi final second leg on 24 April 1975. Leeds had won the first leg at home 2–1, but to a team like Barcelona this was inconsequential. They were coached by the renowned Dutchman, Rinus Michels, and their side, acclaimed as one of the best in the world, included two fellow countrymen, Johann Cruyff and Johan Neeskens, who were liable to tear any team apart on their own, especially in the partisan cauldron of the Nou Camp. No team could possibly feel comfortable about going there with just a one-goal lead. But after just ten minutes of the game, the script went horribly wrong for Barcelona. There seemed little danger to their defence when the Leeds keeper, David Harvey, kicked the ball forward, and even when centre-forward Joe Jordan got his head to it to direct it into the path of another Leeds player around 25 yards from their goal, they could see no reason to panic. But not for nothing was the player concerned – who had been surprisingly left out of the Leeds team for the first leg – known throughout British football as 'hot shot'. He cocked his right foot, and the ball was propelled into the corner of the net like a bullet from a gun.

Peter Lorimer had struck again, and the Barcelona stars, now needing three goals to win the game and clearly getting more dispirited and ragged by the minute, experienced the other side of the Nou Camp coin. The capacity crowd started waving white handkerchiefs, their traditional signal of displeasure against their troops, and Leeds got stronger and stronger. Leeds did concede a goal near the end, after their centre-half, Gordon McQueen, had been sent off. At that point, in a desperate effort to raise the vocal support of their fans to its highest level, Barcelona even played the club's rousing theme song over the loudspeaker system. But the night belonged to Leeds and, of course, to 'hot shot'.

Lorimer, who was with Leeds from May 1962 to March 1979, and returned in December 1983 for another two years at the club at the age of 37, is the only player ever to get 200 goals for them. The youngest-ever first-team debutant for the club, at 15 years and 289 days, the Scottish international scored a total of 238 in 631 first-team matches – 168 goals in the League, 20 in the FA Cup, 19 in the League Cup, 30 in European competitions and one in the Full Members Cup. But his goal in Barcelona will always stand out as the special one for him, not because of the technical quality of the strike itself – he got a number of long-range goals like that – but because of the emotive nature of his underlying motivation.

Leeds were determined to do well in the European Cup that season, not so much for themselves, but for Don Revie, who had left the club to become England manager the previous summer. Lorimer had been one of a number of players who had worked under Revie as youngsters, and who had become caught up in his dream of building an Elland Road team as exciting as the Real Madrid side who dominated the European

Cup in the 1950s. To an extent, that dream, which prompted Revie's decision to change Leeds's playing strip from blue and yellow to Real's all white, was brought to life for Lorimer in the Nou Camp stadium. For Barcelona, it was more like the reliving of their worst nightmare – Real, of course, have always been their strongest Spanish rivals.

When he looks back on that match today, Lorimer, a Leeds publican, also remembers the 1962/63 season when, having signed for Leeds in May 1962, he was among the group of apprentices who worked on clearing the Elland Road pitch of the ice and snow that caused a virtual two-month English soccer shutdown. He and the others would sleep at the ground, in the players' lounge, with Revie's backroom staff cooking their meals – and Revie showing them films of Real Madrid's greatest matches. He must also have wondered what it was about the man that caused him to sign for Leeds – then struggling in the Second Division, when he could easily have gone to more successful and glamorous clubs.

Lorimer, an outstanding schoolboy player in his home town of Dundee, puts it down to the man's enthusiasm and drive – his ability to make people believe that his dream was attainable. Revie, who was married to a Scot, and who quickly targeted Scotland as his key recruitment area in his search for Real Madrid-type stars of the future, said: 'We were invariably knocked out of the cup competitions early, so after the the initial two-matches-a-week period, I was able to do a lot of travelling to look at youngsters in Scotland myself. When I spoke to their parents, my selling line was that their lad would have a better chance of making the first team of a small club like Leeds than one like, say, Manchester United. "Anyway," I'd say, "we'll be a big club ourselves in the not-too-distant future." Some of them looked at me as if I was raving mad.' To emphasise the problems he faced, Revie was fond of recounting a visit to the Edinburgh home of John O'Rourke, a striker who went on to play for many years at Hibernian – and experiencing a struggle just to get through the front door.

'The door was opened by his mother, and I introduced myself and asked if I could have a word with her husband about the possibility of signing John for Leeds. You could actually see through to the living-room, and Mr O'Rourke was sitting by the fire, smoking. He just shouted: "Leeds United? What bloody division do they play in?"'

Revie was luckier in the case of Lorimer, albeit with a helping hand from a Scottish police officer. He recalled:

We had been keen on Peter since he started playing for the Dundee boys team at 13. Over the next few years, I often made the journey to Dundee to talk to his parents so that, by the time he was 15 and selected to play in the Scotland–England schools international at Ibrox, I think I'd become almost a member of the family. Peter was due to leave school on the Tuesday after the match, and the arrangement was that I would go to Dundee immediately after our regular Monday board meeting to sign him. Our chairman Harry Reynolds and I were present at the game [which Scotland won 4–3] and afterwards, we accompanied Peter and his parents to the station to see them on the train back to Dundee. As the train was pulling out, though, who should I see running down the platform to get on it but Tommy Docherty [then Chelsea manager]. I knew he was after Peter, too, and I shouted to him: 'Tommy, you've got no chance.' Tom looked back, smiled and said: 'I'm still going to see what I can do.' It ruined my weekend. Although Peter had agreed to join Leeds, I spent all Sunday afternoon worrying and thinking that I should have got on the train too.

There was an even bigger scare for me on Monday. In the middle of the board meeting, Elsie [his wife] telephoned to say that Lorimer's parents had telephoned to say that Manchester United's Johnny Aston and Joe Armstrong were at their house, and were waiting for Peter to return from a match. They had become quite confused about Peter's future, so Maurice Lindlay [Leeds's chief scout] and I immediately headed north in my old green Morris Oxford. It was very much a race against time, because the last ferry across the Forth was about 10.30 p.m. and we only had three and a half hours to cover the 250 miles to make it. To make it worse, I was stopped for speeding. I told the officer who I was, why I was driving so fast and was virtually pleading with him to be lenient with me. He was, with the result that we were able to reach the ferry just as they were about to lift the drawbridge, and finally arrived at Peter's home near midnight. The Manchester United people had left an hour previously, with the promise that they would be back the following morning. By that time, however, it was too late for them. Peter signed for Leeds at 2.30 a.m. and by 7.30 a.m., the appropriate registration forms were in the post to the Football League.

Lorimer did not have the guile and grace of Leeds's other Scottish winger, Eddie Gray. Moreover, the fact that he scored so many goals might have been viewed as somewhat surprising, because he wasn't the most dangerous of players in the air ('I think I only got two goals with headers') and used his left foot mainly for standing on. But his ability to strike venomous shots, or accurate crosses or long passes, with his right was something else. Quick, strong and intelligent, there was a refreshing simplicity about his game. This, indeed, comes through in the way he analyses it. He admits that, like many other wingers, he never gained as much enjoyment from operating in that position as he would have done in midfield. 'I played up front when I was a schoolboy mainly because of my shot, but I considered my passing was also a strong part of my game. I think Eddie felt the same about being stuck out wide; he, too, would have preferred to be more involved in the game in the middle of the park, but the wide positions were the only ones available to us at Leeds. It's a strange position because you can either get a lot of the ball in a match or be totally starved of it, not get a kick. You find that if a winger clearly has the advantage over the full-back, you get the ball out to him as much as you can. But sometimes, if you're on the other side, you're thinking: "What the hell am I doing out here?" I mean, ask John Giles about playing on the wing – he hated it. And Bobby Collins – it was the same with him.'

Of course, it could have been worse for Lorimer – he could

have been playing out wide in a lesser team than Leeds. 'Yeah,' he agrees, acknowledging the debt he owed to the skill and judgement of men like Bremner and Giles in bringing him into the picture at the right times. 'Teams weren't used to playing against sides of our calibre,' Lorimer says. 'I'd get a full-back who might be thinking: "Oh, there's plenty of space here – I'll let the fellah drop off me five yards." But you couldn't do that with Leeds because people like John – well, they were so accurate with their passing that they could almost part your hair with the ball. He'd just pick it up and – ping. How many other players could do that?' More to the point is the question of how many players could strike the ball as well as Lorimer:

It was natural. It was there from day one. I never worked on my shooting, on trying to hit the ball powerfully. Rhythm and technique came into it, but it was just something that was automatic to me. It's a bit like one player being able to hit the ball better than another in golf. You know, the other week, I was playing with a young pro who has been struggling to keep his head above water on the tournament circuit. He was only a little fellow, not well built or anything like that, but when I saw him hit the ball, I thought: 'Effing hell.' I thought I'd done well to whack it 230 yards, but he was 50 yards in front of me. How could he do that? OK, I am only an average golfer – I play to a ten handicap and I only play maybe once every two or three weeks. But I think part of the answer is natural ability. I think it is like me, with my football. It is just there.

It was a great thing to have in your game. If some players are having a bad game, and they're not goalscorers, then they're in trouble. With me, I could take a couple of free-kicks bang, bang, you put two in and you're a hero. In those days, it was sheer power. The balls used in England were heavier than those of today and when the conditions were wet and muddy, you couldn't make shots bend or dip like you can now. I used to blast my free-kicks as hard as I could straight at the keeper, and people like Billy and Clarkey picked up a lot of goals from rebounds. We knew it was unlikely that the keeper would be able to hold the ball, so when I hit it, we'd have two or three players in specific areas to attack around him to pick up the pieces. Most of the goals I scored in open play came from long range, from just inside or outside the box. Like Eddie, I used to pick up the ball deep, and go at people, and once I was over the halfway line, maybe 30 to 40 yards out, I would start thinking: 'Goal here.' It was quite funny sometimes, in that just when people were starting to give you stick for not passing to them, the ball would be flying into the top corner of the net, so then it would be OK.

The more fundamental secret of Lorimer's success, however, was that in common with the other Leeds players, he played to his strengths. He says: 'Eddie was a totally different player to me. Eddie's game was about dribbling past people, whereas I was a direct player. I could beat someone to get in a cross, but if the cross or pass was on without me having to beat someone, I would do it straightaway. I was lucky in that my range was so good – it was simple for me to knock the ball 30 to 40 yards to clear somebody, and I tried to release the ball as quickly as I could. I mean, I played a very simple game – I think that's the secret of all good teams. I look at some of the amateur teams I play against nowadays [in his capacity as captain of the Leeds ex-players association XI]. If any of our players need to beat someone, they do, but if they don't, they are happy to knock the ball around and do the easy things. When the other team get it they're all trying to do fancy flicks and backheels, things they are not capable of doing. Football is a simple game, that is always the way I have looked at it.'

Well, it wasn't always that simple. Lorimer, for example, is still trying to work out how it was that he didn't score with one of the most cleanly hit shots of his career, in the sensational 1–0 defeat by Sunderland in the 1973 FA Cup final. The Sunderland hero at that moment was goalkeeper Jim Montgomery, who palmed out a shot from the left and then, when Lorimer connected with the rebound in front of an apparently open goal, somehow managed to raise himself quickly enough to deflect the ball onto the bar with an elbow. 'I was only six or seven yards out and I hit it beautifully,' Lorimer recalls. 'As the ball was coming to me, I am thinking: "You don't have to blast it, just a nice contact on the ball will do it." To me, I hit the ball perfectly, just the way I wanted to hit it, and 99 times out of 100, it would have gone in.' The other vital Lorimer goals that got away included his 'equaliser' from a free-kick in the FA Cup semi-final defeat by Chelsea in 1967, which was controversially disallowed by the referee on the grounds that the kick had been taken too quickly; and what would have been the opening goal in the 2–0 1975 European Cup final against Bayern Munich, which was ruled out, just as controversially, because another Leeds player was adjudged to be standing in an offside position.

But Lorimer and Leeds had the character to keep bouncing back from such disappointments. They were also quick learners, a characteristic brought into sharp focus by their European Cup record, and the extent to which their experiences at this level raised the level of 'professionalism' of the team. In learning to extract every possible advantage out of a situation, the lessons Leeds were given were often interpreted as negative. Certainly, they were nothing if not street-wise in such common European football ways as disrupting the momentum of opposing teams through the feigning or exaggeration of injuries, and taking more time than was necessary over corners and throw-ins. Yet, though this antagonised rival fans, and did little to enhance Leeds's public image, nobody could deny that this streak in Revie's XI helped give them a completeness that most other teams lacked.

Revie himself was not averse to playing the gamesmanship game. One of Lorimer's fondest memories concerns an occasion when the manager was beaten at it – in the Fairs Cup semi-final replay against Real Zaragoza in May 1966. Lorimer says: 'The weather was hot and it was at a time in the season when all the pitches were dry and bare. But when we arrived at the ground, he [Revie] says: "You better go out and have a look at the pitch. You'll want a long stud in." I thought: "Long stud? What's he on about?" Well, he'd had the fire brigade down and got them to flood the pitch, hadn't he? "These Spaniards hate conditions like this," he said.' Leeds, however, were thrashed 3–1, and left musing over whether they should have been sorry or glad about Revie's ploy. 'The lads were saying: "Just as well he flooded the effing pitch, otherwise it could have been ten." '

However, Leeds won many more psychological battles than they lost in Europe; and the players under Revie insist that they played a much bigger part in deciding upon their strategy in this department than he did. Billy Bremner put it this way:

I was in the company of an old FA Council member two or three months ago, and he was talking about the bad example the gaffer had set with our team's gamesmanship. 'Don Revie broke the rules,' he said. 'We didn't break the rules – what rules did we break?' I replied. He says: 'Well, he taught you to do this, he taught you to do that,' and I told him that he was talking through his backside; Don Revie never told us to do those things, not once. 'Well, where did you learn them from?' he asked. 'On the Continent,' I said. 'That's where we learned them.'

It's true. We'd play at Elland Road against AC Milan, or Juventus or Barcelona; we'd get a corner, we'd be putting them under pressure, and then suddenly one of their players is down on the floor and we're thinking: 'What's he gone down for?' So they bring the trainer on, and by the time he's gone back to the dug-out and play has resumed, the crowd has quietened down – everything has settled down again. We're thinking: 'Good idea – clever.' It's the same with throw-ins and free-kicks – one player prepares to take it, then someone else comes forward to take it, then someone else. The thing was, when the Continentals did things like that, it was OK, but when British teams did it, it wasn't. You don't break the rules, but you can't be naive. This was one of the great things about that Leeds team in Europe; we just kept picking something up from game to game, from year to year.

Lorimer nods in agreement: 'The other reason why we were a good side was that we couldn't be intimidated. We could play football with the best of them and we could also battle with the best of them. A lot of continental teams are not the same teams when they are away from home, they are totally different to what they are like at home. I remember we played Hungary's Ujpest Dozsa [in the Fairs Cup quarter-final in 1966]. In the first leg at our place, they were jumping out of the way of tackles – they didn't want to know and we beat them 4–1. But in the second leg over there [a 1–1 draw] you couldn't believe it was the same team, you know? They tore us apart. Leeds were different. It didn't matter where we played and who we were playing against, our attitude was always the same.'

There was certainly plenty of evidence of this in that 1–1 draw in Barcelona in 1975, and the ties leading up to it against FC Zurich, Ujpest Dozsa and Anderlecht. All were beaten on their own grounds as well as at Elland Road; and all must have wondered why Leeds, in addition to finishing only ninth in the First Division, lost to Ipswich in the FA Cup sixth round and to Chester in the League Cup third round. 'It was a funny season,' Lorimer recalls, referring to the problems Leeds experienced in adjusting to Revie's departure. To the players and fans, however, the 44-day reign of his successor Brian Clough, which ended with Leeds near the bottom of the table, was no laughing matter:

> Clough was a brilliant manager, no doubt about it, but for me, he cut his own throat at Leeds. He seemed to hate the Leeds set-up. At the first team meeting he had, he told us that as far as he was concerned, we had never won anything fairly and that we might as well throw all the medals we had won in the bin. Then he went through each player and had a go at him. When it was my turn, he said that if I went past the full-back, and was brought down, I tended to make a meal of it to get the full-back into trouble with the referee. I said: 'Well, I remember the stick I got from the Derby full-backs when you

were manager there – if you knocked the ball past them, then bang, they would come in and bury you. Do you expect me to stand for that for the whole game?'

All players have different ways of dealing with situations like that. When Billy was fouled, he'd be up straightaway, and be charging around to get his own back on the player, whereas John would just bide his time. That was the way the game was in those days. It was quite violent. With some of the players you were up against, you really thought: 'I'm going to get clattered today.' Seriously, you really had that feeling in you, and more often than not, you were proved right. So you had to make a meal of it, to make sure you got some protection from the referee and they couldn't do it again without being sent off or booked. It was the only way you could play.

Fortunately for Leeds, a semblance of stability was brought back to the club through the sacking of Clough, and the appointment of the quiet, unassuming Jimmy Armfield as manager. Equally fortunate for them was that the Revie players Armfield had inherited elected to pull together in one last effort to bring Revie's old European Cup–Real Madrid dream to fruition. 'Underneath it all, I think we all knew that this was probably going to be the last season that we would be together,' Lorimer says. 'The Revie team had already started to be broken up, with lads like Frankie Gray, Terry Yorath, Gordon McQueen and Joe Jordan coming through and establishing themselves, and the senior players who were still very much involved – people like myself, Billy Bremner, John Giles, Norman Hunter – were obviously thinking that time was running out for us at the club. The thing that was special about the European Cup to us was that it was the trophy that Don had always most wanted to win. I think much of our motivation in the competition was down to that. We wanted to win it for ourselves, obviously, but we wanted to win it more for the gaffer. I remember the lads were discussing it before the semi-final against Barcelona, and our attitude was: "Come on, it's up to us to do it – let's do it." '

When they did so in the Nou Camp, the most telling picture was provided by the Leeds players, having virtually run themselves to a standstill, finding the energy at the final whistle to do a victory jig in front of the small knot of their supporters. They, in turn, gave a special ovation to Bremner, who in Giles's absence through injury had done enough midfield work for two men; to Jordan, who had laid on the Leeds goal and paid for it with an elbow in the face from a Barcelona player that left a gash in his right eye necessitating five stitches . . . and, of course, Lorimer. Rinus Michels said: 'That early goal shook us so badly that we played nervously until the end of the first half. It was difficult, but not impossible for us to save the match in the second half. We switched to a more English style, but as in many games this season, we could not take our chances.' Perhaps he would have benefited from following the example of Armfield, who upon learning on the eve of the game that Eric Morecambe was in town, had taken the initiative of inviting the comedian to the Leeds squad's hotel to help his troops relax. The comedian did not go far as to give them a rendition of that famous Morecambe and Wise theme song 'Bring me Sunshine'.

But the Leeds fans, and the whole of England, certainly got it when hot shot pulled the trigger.

10

John Lukic

Managers striving to build successful teams start from the back. So when Leeds returned to the First Division in 1990, manager Howard Wilkinson, aware of the importance of having players at this level who can give newly-promoted teams a sense of authority and composure, had no compunction about bringing goalkeeper John Lukic back to the club.

Lukic was not the only Wilkinson signing able to bring these elements into his team – the other was Gary McAllister, who brought an extra touch of class into a Leeds midfield following the departure of a player at the other end of the footballing scale, the notoriously combative Vinny Jones. McAllister, bought from Leicester for £1.2 million, went on to form a midfield triumvirate, with Gordon Strachan and David Batty, that was to evoke memories of the days of Billy Bremner and John Giles. But, for those Leeds fans still clinging to their memories of the top-profile Leeds stars of the past, it would have been difficult to recall any Elland Road goalkeeper quite like John Lukic.

One of the most interesting of Leeds's post-war goalkeeping heroes was Tommy Younger, the former Hibernian and Scotland captain. Younger, who also played for Liverpool and Stoke, was in his thirties and was considered to have gone well past his sell-by date as a top player when Leeds signed him in 1961. Indeed, Younger himself was more than a little surprised to get the chance to prove otherwise, given that he'd been advised to quit playing because of a back problem and, following a spell as a Liverpool publican, left Britain to become coach of a Canadian club. A specialist there, however, had managed to get him playing again and one of his team-mates, Sir Stanley Matthews, recommended him to Revie. The latter recalled: 'I was wary of signing him because, apart from his age, I was told he wasn't a good trainer. But he vowed he would not let me down, and he was true to his word. Tommy weighed fifteen and a half stone when he came to Leeds, but was thirteen stone by the time he started playing for us. He turned in some fantastic displays; in 37 appearances for us, he only conceded about 40 goals. Not only this, he used to return to the ground after training to help coach Gary Sprake. Gary was weak on crosses in those days, in that he tended to take his eye off the ball when challenged physically. It was due mainly to Tommy that he was able to improve this aspect of his game. He devised a practice whereby Gary was repeatedly forced to try and catch high balls – with a medicine ball being thrown at his body.'

Apart from Sprake, who went on to become a Welsh international, the other keeper who distinguished himself under Revie was Scottish international David Harvey, Lukic's predecessor. Lukic was certainly different from those two. Sprake and Harvey operated on a short fuse. Harvey's big-match temperament was better than that of Sprake, whose brilliant natural ability could occasionally be negated by anxiety attacks which led to his being physically sick before games. Harvey, the more vociferous of the two, showed his emotions in other ways. He was a strong character, as he once emphasised when coming to blows with his centre-half, Gordon McQueen, during a game.

In contrast, Lukic, who originally signed for Leeds at 17 in 1978, displaced Harvey at 18 and went on to make a club record 146 successive League appearances before being transferred to Arsenal in 1983, gave the impression of having had a passion by-pass operation. He seemed laid-back almost to the point of being comatose. An intelligent, thoughtful man, with a whimsical sense of humour, he has never been one to subscribe to the late Bill Shankly's view about football being more important than life or death. His ability to put the game, or winning at it, into its proper perspective will have proved somewhat disconcerting to his more blinkered professional colleagues. However, his temperament and personality, combined with the fact that at 6ft 4in he was the tallest keeper in the club's history, meant that there weren't many opposing First Division teams, if any, that his fellow Leeds defenders worried about. In Lukic's first season back at the club, he conceded only 39 goals in 42 matches to help them finish fourth – no mean achievement for a newly-promoted team. It got even better. The following season, he conceded two goals fewer and Leeds won the Championship for the first time in 18 years.

Born and raised in that notable goalkeeper-breeding town of Chesterfield, Lukic, the son of a Serbian labourer, who brought his family to England 'with absolutely nothing', agrees that part of the reason for his part in Leeds's transformation could be attributed to the experience he had gained, especially at Arsenal. He himself had wanted to leave Leeds in 1983 due to a feeling that his career had gone stale there and that he needed a fresh challenge in order to develop further. 'It wasn't just one thing, it was a whole host of things,' he recalls. 'It was quite strange really; I just thought that I had reached the end of the road at Leeds and, without being aware of anyone who was interested in signing me, I asked for a transfer.' In that context, Highbury, where he was able to work with Bob Wilson, the club's goalkeeping coach, not to mention the great Pat Jennings, whom he initially understudied, proved the perfect launching pad for him. Wilson took him on to a new technical plateau. 'What Bob tries to do is to recreate match situations in training,' Lukic explains. 'It's difficult because there are a whole host of unexpected things that go on in a game that you can never anticipate. But that was his basic aim. The main thing, though, was that he put the emphasis on quality rather than quantity. Ultimately, that's what goalkeeping is all about. You don't set your sights on holding five balls out of ten – you can't let one go and think: "Oh, well, the next one will stick." You have got to get one out of one, and that's what Bob's coaching drove home to me.'

After taking over from the similarly cool, calm and collected Jennings as Arsenal's first-choice keeper, Lukic went on to help the Gunners win the League Cup in 1987 and the Championship in 1989. In that championship season, Arsenal conceded 36 goals in their 42 First Division matches. But the most vivid example of Lukic's ability to keep his head under the most intense pressure came in the never-to-be-forgotten last match at Anfield, where the Gunners got the seemingly improbable two-goal win they needed to take the title at Liverpool's expense. A player who has gone through an experience like that should be able to handle anything. So now you know why Lukic was so important to Leeds the second time around:

> You mature as you get older, and things that might have worried you before cease to be a problem. You become more calculating, as opposed to more headstrong, although I don't think I was ever that headstrong or impulsive in the first place. It's quite strange really. You play on sheer enthusiasm when you get into the professional game and then, after a season and a half, you sit back and think: 'Oh right, is this what it's all about?' From that point, you can go one of two ways. You can either slip back, or you can get stronger. The thing is, there is more than one way of getting stronger. You take Peter Schmeichel as an example. He is naturally outgoing and assertive, he expresses his views on a football field in no uncertain terms. That's his way of doing it and that's the way that someone with his make-up can get the best out of himself. I'm not like that, I'm the other way.

162

I've never modelled myself on anybody. I have never looked at anyone and said: 'Oh, I want to be like him.' I think it is essential for you to be true to your own personality, so I've always just done things the way I have wanted to do them. I suppose this was one of the advantages of working with Pat Jennings at Arsenal. By no means did I copy him, and I wouldn't compare myself with him. But he had something in him – this thing about being totally unflappable – that registered with me. I am not a flamboyant goalkeeper. If something can be done just by moving your feet, I do it. I like to do things as easily as I can. You get certain goalkeeping coaches who will come in and say: 'You should do this, you should do that.' If I don't see the necessity for it, I'll say: 'Excuse me, but why?' You know, we're all different. In training, I'll be accused of not diving or really stretching myself to get to the ball, but I don't see why I should do it when the session isn't geared to me. For instance, shooting practice – that's loaded for the strikers, not the goalkeeper.

I don't lose any sleep before games, or anything like that. Big matches don't bother me – it's just a game. It's the same with my reaction to what the crowd and the media might think of me. You could get really neurotic if you listened to everything that people say about you when you concede a goal. I know when I've had a bad game, when I have dropped a ricket. It might be only a split-second thing that you managed to get away with, and which most people did not notice, but I don't need anybody to draw my attention to it anyway. It can be galling sometimes when a TV pundit says something like: 'Oh, the goalkeeper should have moved his feet a bit quicker, he should have got that ball.' As soon as somebody strikes a ball, you have to make an instant judgement, and sometimes your judgement can be proved wrong by circumstances beyond your control. Take the balls that are used nowadays. I remember a match against Aston Villa at Leeds, when Mark Draper hit one from 30 yards. Now, all I had to do was make an easy dive to my right, but as I am about to step across – remember, my weight is going to the right – the ball has swerved, hit my left shoulder and gone on to the crossbar. People say to you: 'What were you doing there?' You try to explain: 'Well, it wasn't me, it was the ball,' but at the same time, you're thinking:

'Am I going crackers?' So I don't believe in getting myself screwed up.

I don't play football just for the sake of it. I play to win, and I do the best that I possibly can. Having said that, I have never felt the need to be constantly reminded about the game. That's why I never lived in Leeds. I liked to go to Elland Road in the morning, and do my thing in training, and I also liked to walk away from it.

There's not a lot that really winds me up on a football field, There has been only one occasion that I have lost my rag with someone on a football field; an opposing player who shall remain nameless. What upset me was that the thing [his foul on Lukic] was premeditated. Other than that, I actually welcome the physical contact side of the game, because I think that the game would lose a lot as a spectator sport if you took this out of it. As a goalkeeper, you have to accept that people will try to upset you, that you will get knocked about, and this has certainly never bothered me one iota. I think I have been too focused on the actual football side to get involved in all of that. That's the way I have been right throughout my career – you set your mind on what you are going to do, and do it. That's it.

The irony of Lukic's return to Elland Road was that it was prompted by Arsenal's signing of David Seaman, once well behind him in the Elland Road goalkeeping pecking order, from QPR. Lukic is characteristically philosophical about his surprise departure from Highbury. On his relationship with the manager, George Graham, he says: 'I have never had what you might call a close relationship with a manager. I'm one of these people who just go in, train or play, and go away. I keep myself to myself, almost to the point where I suppose I might be accused of being anti-social.' He adds: 'Football's a game of opinions. I think there's a passage in George Graham's book where he said that contract negotiations with me were like having teeth pulled. I honestly don't know whether he considered me to be a thorn in his side or not, but he obviously thought that buying David would improve his team. Yes, it probably was a kick in the groin for me, but the reaction I got from the Arsenal supporters compensated for it. They made me feel as though they wanted me to stay, which was nice. That really wasn't an option as far as I was concerned, though. It was obvious that David was going to come into the first team, and for me, getting on my bike and doing something else was preferable to just sitting around and doing nothing. I wasn't worried about the situation – why worry about something you can't change? It might sound blasé, but my attitude was: "Que sera sera." '

That was again his view in the 1996 close season, when Lukic, having been given a free transfer from Leeds, headed back to London for a second spell with Arsenal – as Seaman's understudy.

Blasé? It brings us back to the point that there are worse things in life than losing football matches, and that as far as his Leeds career was concerned Lukic found a manager on the same thoughtful, level-headed wavelength as himself in Howard Wilkinson. Those who have got close to Wilkinson, close enough to look beyond the image he has created for himself through the direct style and high-octane physical output of so many of his teams, indicate that he is a cut above most other managers, intellectually. He has a more academic background for a start, having gained a university degree in PE, and he once spent two years combining the managership of non-leaguers Boston United with a full-time job as an English teacher at his old school in Sheffield. As reflected by his outside interests, such as the writing of humorous fiction stories, he also takes a broader and more balanced view of life. Thus, for this reason alone, there was no danger of Wilkinson and Lukic not being compatible.

Of course, Lukic, like most players working under a new manager, did have one or two adjustments to make. The first concerned Wilkinson's renowned heavy physical training methods. 'Yeah, next question,' Lukic says, smiling. 'On my first day, I was told that I had to do eight laps of a track in 12 minutes, and I thought: "Well, that doesn't sound too bad."

But when I thought more about it, I realised that this was the equivalent of two six-minute miles. That was in the morning. Then, having got through it, there was a 40-minute run in the afternoon. I thought: "What the bloody hell's going on here?" However, I did mellow.' The other adjustment concerned the differences between Arsenal and Leeds in their defensive styles of play. At Arsenal, Lukic was used to operating behind a flat back four which, under the command of captain Tony Adams, liked to push forward as a unit and squeeze the play. It was a system that Lukic says he enjoyed:

> All football is enjoyable when you are winning. Under Terry Neill [the manager who signed him for his first spell at Arsenal], our goals-against record wasn't as good as it probably should have been. I can remember clearly the change that took place when George Graham became manager [in December 1983]. His whole approach was: 'This is the way to defend and I'll teach you how to do it.' It was good for me because, like all goalkeepers, there is nothing I like more than keeping clean sheets. People ridiculed Arsenal for being a boring team, especially with the way they kept catching opponents offside, but there is an art in it, and if opponents didn't have the intelligence to find a way around it, then whose fault was that?
>
> The set-up in the Arsenal defence was very methodical and regimented. You could almost relate to the other defenders with your eyes shut because you knew exactly what they would be doing, where they would be, in various situations. It was slightly different at Leeds, perhaps less regimented. Without going into the nitty-gritty of it, the main adjustment for me was to get used to defenders coming a bit closer to me. When you don't have anybody in your box, the decisions become easier, but as soon as people start backing in, the time you have to make those decisions decreases. I didn't mind this because, as I said, winning football is enjoyable football.
>
> At any event, I couldn't have changed it even if I had wanted to do so. The ultimate responsibility for how a team play, is down to the manager, and you can't say: 'Hold on a second, boss, you've got your head up your backside.' Well, you can – some do – but at the end of the day, you are still left with what

he wants to do. I think you've just got to accept that people have different ways of doing it, and as it was proved, the way the Leeds team was set up was right for the team.

In view of the pressure they were under to gain a foothold in the First Division, and revive the Revie glory days, it was also right for Leeds that they had a goalkeeper with the temperament of Lukic. As a keeper who did not believe in making a meal out of saves, Lukic is remembered more for his biggest mistake – in the European Champions Cup second-round tie against Rangers at Ibrox on 21 October 1992, when he lost sight of the ball in the glare of the floodlights and allowed an Ally McCoist cross to slip from his hands and into the net for an embarrassing own goal. McCoist got one of his own in a 2–1 Rangers victory, which they extended to 4–2 on aggregate in the second leg at Elland Road. However, Lukic's greatest Leeds game, in terms of shot-stopping, was against VFB Stuttgart in the previous round. For the second leg at Elland Road, Leeds, 3–0 down from the first leg, were given the most fervent backing from the crowd that anyone associated with the club could recall. Don Warters, the *Yorkshire Evening Post* football correspondent, recalls: 'The atmosphere at Elland Road was at fever pitch. The support for the team was never quite like that, even for Wembley cup finals.' Leeds responded with a remarkable 4–1 win, and, with his team inevitably stretched at the back in their desperation for goals, Lukic, too, responded superbly through three great point-blank saves from Water, Maurizio and Gaudino. The result should have put Stuttgart through on the away-goal rule, but of course Leeds were awarded the tie 3–0 by UEFA because the German club had mistakenly broken the rules by fielding an ineligible player; and in the replay in Barcelona, they were made to pay an even heavier price for it with a 2–1 defeat.

Dramatic stuff, but not to Mr Super Cool John Lukic. Ask him about his most memorable Leeds performance and he just shrugs. It all boils down to what the great Peter Shilton described as the 'other, unsung side' of goalkeeping – the part that a keeper can play in his team's success just through his personality, his temperament and his presence.

As Shilton once said: 'Some of my best matches have probably been those in which I've hardly had to make a save.'

11

Lee Chapman

Ask Leeds United fans to select the most exciting strikers in Howard Wilkinson's teams, and the chances are that they will give you just two names. One is Tony Yeboah, the explosive Ghanaian who was signed by Wilkinson from Eintracht Frankfurt in January 1995 and whose goal in the early weeks of the 1995/96 season, that astonishing Exocet missile-type long-range shot against Liverpool, has gone down as one of the greatest ever seen in the Premiership. The other, of course, is Eric Cantona, whose touches of genius gave Leeds the extra dimension they needed to clinch the 1992 Championship.

However, there is a third striker who deserves to be on this list. But if you were to mention him in the same breath as Cantona to any member of the Elland Road faithful, the response would be less than convivial.

His name is Lee Chapman, and on the premise that any dream team needs to have plenty of attacking options – they can't always play fantasy football with exquisite passing and dribbling – then he's a must. Chapman is the big, blond, occasionally clumsy-looking centre-forward who, while not possessing the talent of a Yeboah or a Cantona, was nonetheless ideally suited to Wilkinson's direct style of play. Yeboah and Cantona might be able to show him a thing or two about ball-playing skills, but there were few who could match his power in the air.

This aspect of his game, combined with his positional instincts for scoring chances, brought the underrated Chapman some 62 goals in 137 League matches. After being signed from Sheffield Wednesday towards the end of the 1989/90 season, his 12 goals in 21 matches pushed Leeds to the Second Division Championship. He was their top scorer when they finished fourth in the First Division in 1991 and again when they won the First Division title in 1992. Unfortunately for Chapman, though, Leeds fans tend to view this record with mixed feelings. It was Cantona who was their idol, and they will forever remember Chapman's involvement in the bust-up which led to the Frenchman's transfer to Manchester United and, as a consequence, the greatest run of success in United's history. Indeed, some argue that had it not been for Chapman's presence at Elland Road, Cantona – who in his short spell there became one of the most feted stars Leeds have ever had – might well have remained and done for them what he has done for their fierce Lancashire rivals. Of course, the main factor behind Cantona's departure was the clash in football mentalities and ideas between him and Wilkinson. As has been well documented through the public pronouncements on this unhappy marriage from both parties, the temperamental Cantona demanded more freedom of expression and power than the dour, pragmatic Wilkinson was prepared to give him. As far as the footballing side of his Leeds career was concerned, the major Cantona problem for Wilkinson was that Leeds, with their rigid style of play, did not present the best platform for the Frenchman to fully exploit his skills. Thus, Wilkinson faced the dilemma of either trying to force Cantona to adapt to Leeds or rebuilding the Leeds team so that they could adapt to him.

This is where Chapman came in. Leeds had achieved their success on fitness, physical strength and organisation. In the latter respect, they used a basic, straightforward system in which midfield inter-play was deemed secondary to getting the ball into the opposing danger areas as early as possible. Leeds played what can best be described as a refined long-ball game and Chapman's qualities as a 'target man' centre-forward made him its ideal attacking focal point.

Not surprisingly, though Wilkinson rightly perceived Cantona as someone who could provide the extra sparkle and ingenuity to Leeds's play when he signed him – initially on loan from the French club, Nimes, in January 1992, he was loath to tamper with the basic chemistry of his team. Cantona's individuality, combined with the fact that he had not played competitive football for six months, caused Wilkinson to use him mainly as a substitute for Leeds's last 15 matches. The atmosphere this created between Wilkinson and Cantona – and, indeed, Chapman and Cantona – and what it led to is one of the most absorbing passages in an intriguing book on Cantona [*Cantona, the Red and the Black*] written by Ian Ridley of the *Independent on Sunday*. On the initial problems of Cantona settling down in the team, Chapman, ironically Cantona's room-mate on Leeds away trips, is quoted as saying: 'We played a very direct sort of game and I was the target man. The ball was played quite early up to me and people fed off me. Eric really prefers to play between the midfield and the forwards. But we didn't play like that, so he tended to be overlooked all the time. Eric really came into his own when the pace of the game had cooled down a bit and there was lots of space developing.'

The following season, Wilkinson, conscious of the need for Leeds to build on their Championship breakthrough by doing well in the European Cup and Champions League, decided to give Cantona greater scope to be himself by modifying the team's style, and encouraging more of a passing game. As indicated by Leeds's indifferent results, they appeared to lose much of their effectiveness. But Wilkinson, under pressure to play Cantona and having apparently been told by the Frenchman that he was finding it difficult to play with Chapman, responded by dropping Chapman for the match against Manchester City on 7 November. Chapman told Ridley: 'I'd had one of my best starts to a season for some time, and I was left out. I was shocked when I found out why later, because I wouldn't be capable of doing something like that. But Eric is very single-minded, and if he isn't in control of the situation, and if it isn't all revolving around Eric, then he finds it difficult to play second string.' Leeds were beaten 4–0 by City, and that was Cantona's last League appearance for them. On 26 November 1992, he was transferred to Manchester United. Chapman went on to help Leeds avoid relegation by again finishing their leading goalscorer, with 14, before being transferred to Portsmouth in the summer.

In his interview with Ridley, Chapman claimed that Leeds would not have been in that trouble in the first place had they avoided the temptation to change their style of play to suit Cantona. And as for Cantona's influence on the side in their Championship-winning season, he said: 'I think Eric's contribution has been overrated, yes. He was cited as one of the reasons why we won the title, but he only joined us in January, half the season had already gone and we were still in a strong position at the time. When he started a game, he didn't make much of a contribution because he hadn't adjusted to the pace. It was only really when he came on as a substitute in the later stages that he really contributed. I think they overestimated what he contributed and that demeans what the rest of the players did. The players who were already there were really the reason why we won it. Of the goals that he scored [against Wimbledon, Luton and Chelsea], only the one against Luton was a decisive goal. We were already ahead when he scored the others.'

It would be easy to dismiss all this as sour grapes, except that Chapman, among the most well-read and erudite of professional footballers, has also been one of the most personable. Chapman, who is married to the actress Leslie

Ash, and whose hobbies include collecting fine wines and writing (he was once a football columnist for the *Observer* newspaper) can certainly have no misgivings about his own contribution to Leeds's Championship cause. Cantona's goal in the 5–1 win over Wimbledon was overshadowed by the fact that Chapman got a hat-trick. He was also on the mark in Cantona's other scoring matches against Luton (2–0) and Chelsea (3–0). He scored 16 in that season, but if there was one match in which his importance to Leeds was brought into particularly sharp focus, it was the one at his old club Sheffield Wednesday on 12 January 1992.

It was a crucial game for Leeds in that earlier that week they had suffered a 3–1 home defeat by Manchester United, their strongest Championship rivals, in the fifth round of the Rumbelows Cup, a setback which their followers feared might have a disastrous psychological effect on their title challenge. But Leeds's response was remarkable. They thrashed Wednesday 6–1, their biggest league away win since September 1930 and Wednesday's heaviest home league defeat in the club's history. And Chapman, revelling in the space Leeds created through the incisive high-speed thrusts of Tony Dorigo and Rod Wallace down the flanks, did most of the damage with a hat-trick.

Eat your heart out, Cantona? Well, maybe that is going too far. But in the Leeds team that Wilkinson created, there can be little doubt that, of these two widely contrasting footballers, Chapman fitted into the jigsaw the best. He did so because it was Wilkinson's jigsaw, the same sort of jigsaw that Chapman had experienced when working with the manager at Sheffield Wednesday. In that respect, it is no coincidence that the point at which Wilkinson bought him for Wednesday, in August 1984, following Chapman's somewhat chequered first six years in the game with Stoke, Plymouth, Arsenal and Sunderland, was the one at which he started to truly assert himself.

The Lincoln-born Chapman, the son of the late Roy

Chapman, a former Aston Villa, Lincoln and Mansfield striker, and Port Vale and Stafford Rangers manager, scored 63 goals in 149 League matches for Wednesday, his most potent form since the start of his career, when he got 34 goals in 99 games for Stoke City. The latter club, where his mother worked as a secretary, was like Utopia compared with his next ports of call. He had lasted only 16 months in the First Division at Arsenal (four goals in 23 matches) and eight months at Sunderland (three in 15). So what was it about Wednesday, and Wilkinson, that stimulated him? The simple answer is that as Chapman's lack of pace and mobility rendered him a rigid type of player, he needed to be in a rigid style of play. He puts it this way: 'The difference was that Howard Wilkinson provided the right framework, the right stability. He is very good at laying down what is required of a player. There are no grey areas – it's either black or white, and you know exactly what your job entails. I don't think I had that at Arsenal and Sunderland. A lot of the managers I have played for have been a bit vague. They have just let you go out on the pitch hoping that it would all gel together. In my case, the starting point for me at Wednesday was to cause havoc in the opposing penalty area and get goals. But the team had to work to strict guidelines. I suppose the best way to put it is that we had a good disciplined shape. When you have that, you all know your roles and it's easier to perform. That's what we had at Sheffield Wednesday, and Leeds. A great shape – everyone knew what he was doing.'

What also helped him was Wilkinson's belief in teams not playing six passes in situations where one would do. The direct style of play of Wednesday and Leeds under Wilkinson's management suited Chapman perfectly. As he was not blessed with the velvet touch and the sharpness in tight areas of stars like Cantona, being in a team that favoured an intricate attacking build-up was the last thing he needed. The archetypal move involving a centre-forward like Chapman was to get to a long ball from his defence, quickly lay it off to a supporting colleague, and then get in the box to apply the finishing touch. The earlier the pass to him, and especially the high pass, the more effective he became. The other thing that served Leeds in good stead was that, as with the wine he collects, Chapman had matured with age by the time he joined forces with Wilkinson again.

In that respect, the other turning point for him was that, previously having joined the French Second Division club Niort only to find that they couldn't afford his modest transfer fee, not to mention his wages, he was 'rescued' by Nottingham Forest's Brian Clough. It was at Forest that, much to his surprise, he found himself playing with the ball as opposed to chasing it or trying to get his head to it by the far post. 'Forest played a lot through the middle – they didn't get ball in from the flanks as much as the other clubs I'd been with – so they wanted me to drop off more and turn with the ball. It was probably the biggest change of style I had experienced. It was difficult to adjust at first. Having the ball played to my feet was one thing. Also, at my previous clubs, I'd been strictly a far-post player, but at Forest, they put everything to the near post. I wondered whether I was capable of playing Forest's way, I must say. But it was a challenge, and I thrive on challenges – I like the pressure. This particular one made me a more accomplished player without a doubt. My touch, my ball control, it improved so much. During that period, I probably did more on the ball than I had done in all my previous years in the game. It set me on my way really.'

Chapman was 30 when he joined Leeds. But he was then at his peak. By that time, he had learnt virtually all of what he describes as the 'tricks of the trade'. He says:

> Centre-forward play is an art form, and the more you play, the more you learn. You know, every player has faults, but there are lots of little tricks of the trade that can help you

hide them. Players can survive a lot longer if they have looked after themselves physically, but the main thing is picking up the knowledge.

The one quality I most regret not having is searing pace. I'm not as slow as people make out, but nevertheless, I have never had the sort of pace that was going to frighten defenders, put it that way. Yet the older I got, the more this was offset by my ability to read a game. My goalscoring improved as I got older, purely and simply because I learned where to be and when to arrive in that position. Football is a game of percentages really. Obviously, a striker has to have a natural instinct for goals, but it's also about knowing what sort of runs are going to bring you the highest percentage of scoring chances. It's a gradual process. You don't suddenly wake up one morning and shout: 'Eureka.' You cannot point to one specific incident or experience as having made you a good footballer; over the years, the lessons that you need to reach this level just filter into you, bit by bit. Even the bad experiences can be important. For example, in hindsight, I would say that what happened to me at Arsenal helped me enormously, because I reached rock bottom – I couldn't go down any further. It was my own fault in one way – I should have waited another two or three years before going to a big city club like that. It wasn't like Liverpool, where players as inexperienced as I was are initially put in the reserves. Terry Neill [then Arsenal manager] was under enormous pressure. He needed a goalscorer in the team, and he just thought that sticking me in would solve the problem. But it didn't. I was naive and immature both on and off the field. Quite honestly, I just wasn't ready to be in a situation like that.

Things went from bad to worse at Sunderland. I only moved there because Alan Durbam, my Stoke manager, was there. But like Terry Neill, he was also under a lot of pressure. He got the sack within weeks of my joining the club, and I thought: 'Oh, here we go again.' However, where I think these experiences helped me was that it shattered my confidence and I had to show a lot of strength of character to recover and build myself up again.

That strength of character, and the knowledge he has acquired, was still serving him in good stead in the 1995/96 season, when he played for Ipswich, and then Swansea (his 12th club) at the age of 37. It seems incongruous that he has not attracted greater public acclaim, but he himself stresses that he is not unhappy about this.

'It's a very insular game,' he says. 'When you go into it from school, you are put into a sort of cocoon. Your club makes all the decisions for you; they tell you when to eat, sleep, train – they tend to shield you from the outside world, the real world. But I have deliberately forced myself away from that. I have learnt from my father. His whole life revolved around football, and eventually it was the cause of his death [at 49]. I think his inability to adjust to life outside football was the main reason why he had a heart attack. That has taught me not to be too dependent on football.' By that, he also means too dependent on the adulation of the crowd. 'The most common comments about me are that I am underrated and that I haven't had the credit I deserve,' he says. 'This doesn't bother me at all. The only things that bother me are how many goals I score, whether my team is winning and how I am looked upon by the manager and my fellow players. That's all I am concerned about.'

There are no prizes for guessing how Howard Wilkinson and Chapman's Elland Road team-mates looked upon him when Leeds won the Championship – and especially on that January afternoon when he spearheaded the destruction of Sheffield Wednesday. What made the win particularly impressive was that Wednesday had gone 14 successive home matches without defeat, and Leeds were without two of their key midfielders, Gordon Strachan and David Batty, through injury. It was a nightmare for Wednesday's Swedish right-back, Roland Nilsson, who was repeatedly beaten for pace by Dorigo and Wallace. But it was even more of one for the men marking Chapman, who scored the first goal with a simple close-range shot after a Gary McAllister corner had been headed on by Chris Whyte. From that moment, there was no stopping Chapman, or Leeds. The extent to which the goal lifted him was seen when he surged forward with the ball, from a deep position, and struck a shot against the bar. There was only a brief period that Wednesday looked as if they might make a game of it, when John Sheridan converted a disputed penalty to make the score 2–1. But just before half-time, the irresistible Chapman struck again with a header from Gary Speed's left-wing cross. He completed his hat-trick with another header, after a Speed effort had hit the woodwork.

It was shortly after that match that Cantona arrived in England to sign for Sheffield Wednesday. Cantona was none too pleased when Wednesday suggested that he spend a week on trial with them to allow both parties to assess each other, and his mood grew darker still when the club requested a one-week extension to the arrangement. Hence Cantona's move to Leeds.

Wednesday have long insisted that their attitude towards Cantona was the right one at that time. No doubt, any sense of loss they experienced over the Frenchman that season was nothing compared with what they felt like at not having a Lee Chapman.

12

Gordon Strachan

'Look at me,' says Gordon Strachan, drawing your attention to the unimpressive physique encompassed in his 5ft 6in frame. 'I don't look like an athlete – I don't even look like a football player.'

All of which highlights how deceptive appearances can be. As both an athlete and a footballer, Strachan, who played for Leeds from the age of 32 to 38, has to go down as one of the all-time Elland Road greats; without doubt, one of the precious few players before or after the Don Revie era who would have looked entirely comfortable in Revie's outstanding sides. In many ways, Strachan, with his sharp football brain and superb first touch, was the Leeds midfielder who came closest to matching the inspiration provided by Billy Bremner. Like Bremner, he has red hair and is a Scottish international. Indeed, at the start of his career with Dundee, one local newspaper headline proclaimed: 'Strachan is the next Bremner'. That did not turn out to be strictly true because Strachan, though strong-minded and possessing a fiery streak, was not as physically combative as Bremner. Nonetheless, he was similar in terms of his creative skills and his attitude to the game. Like Bremner, he appeared to play on an inexhaustible supply of energy and enthusiasm, often creating or scoring a goal when it was most needed. During his six years at Leeds, Strachan picked up more 'man of the match' awards than any other player, and won the Footballer of the Year award in 1991.

In view of the age at which he joined Leeds, and his part in helping to transform the club's fortunes, one could also draw a parallel with another Scottish midfielder, Bobby Collins, who was signed from Everton and did so much to steer Leeds out of the Second Division and to the top of the First in the mid-1960s. As with Collins, Strachan appeared to be approaching the end of his career at the top level when he signed for Leeds in March 1989, just five months after Howard Wilkinson's arrival there as manager. He had spent seven years at Manchester United, five of them under the management of Alex Ferguson, who had previously worked with him at Aberdeen for six years. Yet, like Collins, Strachan took on a new lease of life at Elland Road. In so doing, he highlighted the advantages of players adopting the right diet – in his case, bananas, porridge, pasta, fish and chicken supplemented by seaweed tablets – and the methods of a Norwegian stress counsellor by the name of Harold Oyen. He says that part of his knowledge on how to maintain his fitness, and even improve it, as he got older stemmed from his association with players like Graeme Souness, who had been subjected to the highest body-care and maintenance standards when playing for clubs in other countries. Kenny Dalglish, another fellow member of the Scotland squad, also had an influence on him through his determination to use his free time between training and matches to get plenty of rest and sleep.

But the two men who have influenced him the most are tennis player Ivan Lendl, and Oyen. In his latest book (*Strachan Style – A Life in Football*), Strachan – who left Leeds to rejoin his old United boss Ron Atkinson at Coventry, as assistant manager – explained: 'I was watching the tennis on TV one day and I saw Ivan Lendl eating one [a banana] during a break in his game. I thought to myself, if he is doing that, then it must be because it is good for him and will be providing him with the energy he needs to compete at the top level. When you check it out, you find that bananas have a very high vitamin count, containing vitamins A, B and C. They are very nutritious, and yet low in calories – in fact ideal for any sportsman. So I now breakfast every day on porridge and bananas, and that's my start to the day. It's a high energy, low fat beginning, and I try to keep to that kind of healthy eating every day and right through the week. I cannot remember the last time I ate any chips or fried food, or any kind of junk food at all. I have tried to ease myself away from the kind of meals which I felt were not doing me any good.' As for Oyen, he said: 'As well as diet and training, I am into biokinetics [the art of maintaining the flow of energy through the body by fingertip pressure on certain points] and there is this expert in this field, a Norwegian called Harold Oyen, who looks after me. He works on stress management and I met him when I was at Manchester United. I got to know him through the Manchester United director and former player Bobby Charlton, who was endorsing seaweed tablets. I was fascinated by his ideas on fitness. I can do this [fingertip pressure] to some extent on myself now, and I have a little ritual that I go through in the dressing-room before training and games. I sit there and give myself a little massage in certain places. When I first got to Leeds, I think some of the players felt I must be potty. They must have taken a look at me sitting there pushing and prodding away at these different pressure points and thought: "We've got a right one here." '

They had good cause to change their minds on that one, though, as Strachan went on to play 120 first-team matches on the trot, all but one for the full 90 minutes. 'That can't be bad for someone in his thirties,' he reminds you. 'I would have liked to get on to these sort of things earlier in my career. But, when I started, the knowledge and expertise on subjects like diet in professional football wasn't as widespread as it is now. In any case, when I started at Dundee at the age of 15, I was only getting £13 a week, or £9 if you take away the money I was paying for my digs, and there weren't many places where pasta was on the menu. In those days footballers, while earning more money than the average working man, did not get that much more. In recent years, the gap has become unbelievable, and players know that if they can reach the top and stay there, just for five or six years, then they can set themselves up financially for the rest of their lives. So there are a lot of players who have started thinking more seriously about their fitness, not just me.

'People get the wrong idea when I try to get over the importance of staying fit. When your stamina goes, your concentration goes, too, that's when you start to make mistakes. So, when I talk about fitness, I don't mean the ability to run about like a madman; I am talking about keeping your skill-level high.'

In the case of Strachan, the skill-level was as high as that of anyone. Ferguson drooled over his first touch, and his competitiveness, although there was some conflict between the two men on the question of the role to which he was best suited. Strachan wanted to play in the centre of midfield, whereas Ferguson preferred to use him on the right. Recalling his success at Aberdeen, Ferguson said:

> Perhaps the most important decision I made came after a 1–0 defeat in a pre-season match at Kilmarnock, where we had started with a midfield of Sullivan, Strachan and Jarvie. I realised I would need to decide finally where to play Strachan. He was a talented player, had a marvellous temperament, wanted to play and was prepared to be on the ball all the time. But I became sure that we were really wasting his talents by playing him in central midfield because he played too many short balls from that position. He was also easily nailed by the more physical players in that area. We couldn't expect him to win tackles against men like Roy Aitken and Tom Forsyth, so I decided to play him on the right side.
>
> We then saw Gordon flourish and become the great player of later years. It was as if he had sprouted wings. I had admired him as a player at Dundee. I always admire players with ability, good control, good vision, a sort of cheeky arrogance.

People always ask me what Gordon's greatest asset is, and I always say it is his first touch of the ball. No matter which angle the ball comes to him or whatever its pace, Gordon will control that ball immediately. Another thing that people often overlook is that he is a good finisher, a high quality finisher. We used to urge him to operate up the park as much as possible because he was always capable of scoring a goal. If you think about it, in his six seasons with me, he scored 90 goals. For a midfield player, that's not bad going at all.

Most players would be ecstatic over a reference like that, but Strachan's pride is such that even now, he finds it difficult to avoid reacting to what he perceives as misconceptions about him. For example, nothing rankles with him more than his being described as a 'right winger'. He seems irritated, too, when you bring up Ferguson's point about his emphasis on short passes. 'I would always be looking to play the longer, more telling pass,' he says, 'but you often have to play the short stuff first to be able to draw people in and create the necessary space.' He pauses, and reminds you that as a member of Scotland's team when Andy Roxburgh was national coach, Roxburgh went on record as describing him as one of the best players in the game at hitting long, diagonal passes to open up the play and change the direction of an attack. Suffice it to say that Strachan can also come up with a pretty powerful argument to disprove Ferguson's point about his physical power, through his record of 600 League appearances on both sides of the border; his relative shortage of serious injury problems; and the thought that few opponents have been able to get close enough to him to be able to change this.

When discussing that Strachan pride, Ferguson himself is fond of recalling a clash between the two men at Aberdeen, when the manager, anxious to show the less important members of his team that nobody was excepted from getting a tongue-lashing from him, deliberately picked on Strachan at a team meeting. Ferguson took the precaution of pulling Strachan aside beforehand, to tell him what he was going to do and why, and Strachan himself agreed to play along with it. But Strachan still couldn't help taking exception to some of Ferguson's criticisms of him and the two men ended up having a fierce row – for real.

In truth, the relationship between Ferguson and Strachan always had a volatile element. It was a disagreement with Ferguson that almost led to Strachan making the biggest mistake of his life. It happened in 1984 when Ferguson, resigned to losing him to a bigger club when his Aberdeen contract expired at the end of the season, dropped him for a match against Hearts. This was followed by Strachan explaining why he felt the decision was wrong in his regular newspaper column; Ferguson demanding that the column be stopped; and then Strachan signing an agreement, through an agent and without Ferguson's knowledge, to join Cologne.

Some time later, in his book on his Aberdeen days, Ferguson recalled: 'It wasn't until we had agreed a deal for Gordon's transfer to Manchester United, and told the player, that he informed us that he had signed a contract with Cologne. I was thunderstruck. I said: "What do you think you are doing, going to a club like Cologne? Last year, they were playing to crowds of about 3,000 in some games. You need a big platform – that's why you're leaving Aberdeen in the first place." Eventually, though, we found that the document had no legal validity, and no one was more relieved about that than the wee man himself.'

Strachan, endorsing Ferguson's assertion that 'footballers respond to anger', agrees that Ferguson's abrasive, confrontational style of management at Aberdeen and his early days at Manchester United helped bring the best out of him. But there had to come a time when the chemistry between them would start to lose its potency. In the months leading up to his departure from Old Trafford, Strachan sensed that his days at Old Trafford were numbered – he had learned that Ferguson was searching for someone to replace him – and was in no way unhappy about the prospect of leaving. For his part, he felt that the two men had got to know each other almost too well and that he needed a new challenge.

That new challenge was provided through his finding a manager, Howard Wilkinson, willing to give him the responsibility – and the respect – that he felt his background in the game merited. Certainly, Strachan does not disagree when you suggest to him that Ferguson, through having worked with him since the early part of his development, might have been too close to him to be able to fully appreciate what he had to offer. 'I was part of the furniture at Old Trafford,' he says. In a sense, Strachan felt that he had become too marginalised at Old Trafford, just as he felt he had been marginalised through being stuck out on the right flank instead of in the hub of the action in the middle of the field.

In that respect, the difference in Wilkinson's attitude towards him stemmed from the fact that, whereas he had initially joined forces with Ferguson as a raw youngster, he linked up with Wilkinson as an established high-profile star.

Wilkinson, badly needing someone of Strachan's stature to help raise the professional standards and skill-level of his then Second Division team, made Strachan team captain. Indeed, Wilkinson left nobody in any doubt that Strachan was going to be his manager on the field. Strachan says: 'Leeds were exactly the type of club I was looking for – a big club which had fallen on hard times and needed some help. I couldn't help but admire what Howard was trying to do. There had been a number of players there who were what I would call football nomads. They were just happy to stay there for a year or two, pick up their money and go. Howard changed all that. He brought in players who badly wanted to play for the club, who had pride in the club. I think I got closer to him than I did to any of my other managers because he treated me like a man. He brought me into things. He gave me more responsibility. I couldn't help but react to that.'

There is a telling insight on this in Strachan's book, published when he was still at Leeds: 'He [Wilkinson] looks for leadership by example, and that's what I try to give him. He's not daft. He knows how I live my life, and he wants me to pass some of the things I have learned on to the younger lads. I take my captain's duty pretty seriously. For instance, at the start of every season, I give the lads a little talk and tell them what is expected of them at the club. It's good fun. It's informal and it's humorous, and I think that helps the lads relax a bit. They don't feel scared or overawed as they might do if it was the manager laying down the law. This is me, just one of the players, and all I do is lay down guidelines for them to follow.'

Initially, it seemed strange to say the least to find a ball-player like Strachan establishing such an effective rapport with Wilkinson, given Wilkinson's reputation for producing football devoid of frills. This pragmatic streak in the man was certainly evident when Leeds were in the Second Division, as seen by his signing of Vinny Jones. It has often been said that the best chance teams have of lifting themselves out of that environment is to put the emphasis on physical strength, determination and organisation, rather than silky skills, and Wilkinson was not the sort of figure to attempt to prove otherwise. However, though Strachan was forced to be more direct, and spend more of his time looking for possession in and around the opposing penalty area instead of setting up the play in deeper positions, he insists that this did not go as much against the grain for him as some might have imagined:

> People have certain ideas about Howard, but once you actually sit down and talk to him about his methods, you are totally blown away. As a youngster, you tend to think there is only one way to play the game, but as you get older, you do become more open-minded. He made me appreciate that whatever the system of style of a team, it has to create scoring chances. You can string as many lovely passes together as you want, but if it doesn't result in a scoring chance, it's a waste of time. As for the long-ball stigma, he also drove it home to me that there is a big difference between a long pass, which is what he

likes to see, and a long hoof up the park. You know, if someone like Ruud Gullit hit a long pass, people would say: 'Oh, great ball.' If one of Howard's players did it, the reaction would be: 'Just like Wimbledon.' Basically, Howard said that there was a certain way of playing that would get us out of the Second Division, provided that we trusted his judgement enough to work at it. We did trust him and it did work. He didn't say 'I don't want you to play,' but first we had to pressurise teams, wear them down. He convinced me that he knew what he was doing, and it was the same with the others.

Over the next two seasons, when Leeds finished fourth in the First Division and then won the Championship, Strachan, part of a midfield unit incorporating the ball-winning qualities of David Batty, the surging, incisive forward runs of Gary Speed and the elegant skills of his fellow Scottish international Gary McAllister, enjoyed himself even more. McAllister (now with Strachan again, at Coventry) was signed by Wilkinson from Leicester in July 1990, and Strachan points out: 'Our understanding was almost telepathic. I think I lost count the number of times that I would come towards him, "showing" for a ball to be played to my feet, and then suddenly spin around the defender tracking me and have the ball played by Gary into the space behind. It was the same with little one-twos between us and things like that – we thought alike.

'I think that when Gary joined, some felt that we might get in each other's way. But this was never the case. We both knew that there were going to be games when I would be on song, and he wouldn't be, and vice versa, but the main thing was that we supported each other 100 per cent.'

For his part, McAllister must have been relieved to have Strachan playing with him, rather than against him. For example, one of Strachan's most memorable Leeds performances came in the 2–1 win over McAllister's Leicester in Leeds's last home match of their 1989/90 Second Division Championship-winning season. Three days earlier, Leeds had suffered a shock 2–1 home defeat by Barnsley. With two games left, they were level on points with Sheffield United at the top of the table, with Newcastle just two points behind. Thus, promotion was very much in the balance, let alone the title. After taking a first-half lead against Leicester through Mel Sterland, Leeds put their fans through an emotional torture chamber by conceding a McAllister equaliser. It got even worse as Leeds, driven on by Strachan, missed a succession of chances and McAllister came close to putting them 2–1 down with a shot brilliantly saved by Mervyn Day.

Far from wilting under this pressure, however, Strachan – looking as if he had eaten a whole boat-load of those bananas in one day – just seemed to get stronger and stronger. 'I don't think I have ever put more into a game than I did in the last 20 minutes of that match,' he recalls. Near the end, he and Leeds got their reward when a mistake just outside the Leicester box, ironically by McAllister, led to Strachan hitting in a glorious 20-yard drive (uncharacteristically with his left foot). Wilkinson has said that he has never seen a player look so pale and drawn after scoring a goal as Strachan did. 'When I saw the TV pictures of the players lifting me up on the touchline, I thought I looked skeletal,' Strachan recalls. 'I was so tired that I actually fell asleep on the journey home.'

However, to get an even fuller flavour of Strachan's leadership qualities, the incredible energy he put into his play, it is necessary to wind the memory video forward – to 10 April 1993 and Leeds United's home match against Blackburn. With seven matches to go, Leeds had dropped from 13th to 16th in the table, just four places above the relegation zone. Only five points separated them from the third-from-bottom club Oldham, and they had to face an in-form Blackburn team (chasing a place in Europe) without McAllister, Batty and Tony Dorigo. But the good news was they could at least call on Strachan, who had issued a stirring rallying call to his Elland Road troops earlier in the week – and then proceeded to show that he had got the message loud and clear himself with a hat-trick in a resounding 5–2 Leeds win.

The usually dour Wilkinson was moved to describe him as 'Captain Courageous', adding: 'Leadership was required, and he gave it in every respect. He played like a leader, fought and chased like one, gave praise when it was necessary and criticism when that was required. He was magnificent.' The *Yorkshire Evening Post* hailed his performance as a master class: 'After watching Gordon Strachan almost single-handedly tear Blackburn's defence into little pieces, a horrible thought sprung to mind. What will Leeds United do when he has to admit that time has caught up with him? The enthusiasm, skill, leadership and aggression that make him a cut above any of his Premier League peers are qualities Leeds cannot afford to lose.' Leeds's penalty takers then were McAllister and Dorigo, but with both absent, Strachan emphasised his willingness to accept responsibility by taking the early spot kick, awarded for a foul on Lee Chapman, and scoring from it. Strachan made it 2–0 from another penalty, after he himself had been brought down by Stuart Ripley. His third goal was somewhat more spectacular – a clever exchange of passes with Jamie Forrester, followed by a thunderbolt of a shot into the top corner of the Blackburn goal from 20 yards. The same could be said of his part in Leeds's fourth goal, when he played a perfect, long, high pass into the path of Rod Wallace.

The following Monday, the acclaim of the Strachan show in the *Yorkshire Evening Post* was accompanied by a report on the concern among Leeds United bond-holders about whether they would get the best seats in the new East Stand. United's chairman, Leslie Silver, issued a public invitation for the disgruntled followers to turn up at Elland Road the following morning. He said: 'Come up with me and sit in the stand and look down, and I can assure you it will be a real experience to see football played from that position.'

But it was a real experience to see it from any position when Gordon Strachan was playing for Leeds. When Ferguson joined him at Manchester United, he had greeted him with the words: 'Hello, ugly.' He was only joking, of course, as Leeds fans would readily confirm. Ugly? At Leeds, little Strachan, with his red hair and ungainly-looking physique, was a thing of rare football beauty.

Depending on your football tastes, the same could also be said of the likes of John Charles, Norman Hunter, Paul Reaney, Billy Bremner, John Giles, Allan Clarke, Peter Lorimer, Eddie Gray, John Lukic and Lee Chapman.